ADDISON WESLEY LONGMAN HISTORY IN DEPTH SERIES

19

OLIVER CROMWELL AND THE CIVIL WAR AND INTERREGNUM

James Mason and Angela Leonard
Series editor: Christopher Culpin

Nadia. Outer 13s.

GW00597478

LONGMAN

CONTENTS

PART ONE

TELLING THE STORY

Few figures in British history stir up so many passions as Oliver Cromwell. In 1960 Wallingford Borough Council banned a proposal to call a road on a new housing estate Cromwell Gardens. 'We have more than enough benefactors whose names we would like to commemorate without entertaining a malefactor in his class,' they told the *Oxford Mail*. A hundred years earlier, in another Oxfordshire village, mothers would frighten naughty children with the threat, 'Old Crummell'll have 'ee'. Yet, at the time, people in the West Riding of Yorkshire were using the phrase 'In Oliver's days' to describe a time of exceptional prosperity.

Cromwell became the leading player on the mid-seventeenth century political stage at a time of high drama and conflict in England and Wales, Scotland and Ireland. It is hardly surprising, therefore, that people at the time should have held contrasting views of him. To his admirer, the poet John Milton, he was 'Our Chief of Men'; to his royalist enemies, and even to some of his one-time allies who felt betrayed by him, he was an ambitious schemer, an evil hypocrite, 'The English Devil'. The best that could be said of him by a royalist was said by the Earl of Clarendon who pronounced him, 'a brave, bad man'.

Controversy has raged ever since. In the last 200 years historians have portrayed him variously as a revolutionary prepared to do away with his king, a representative of a rising middle class standing for religious freedoms and the rights of parliament, a conservative who did not believe in revolution and crushed those who did, a dictator, a reluctant dictator, and an anguished Christian seeking to discover and act upon the will of God.

Little about Oliver Cromwell was simple or straightforward. This book aims to help you to examine the actions and motives of a fascinating and complex individual. It also helps you to enquire into some of the issues surrounding the extraordinary career of a man who, in middle age, emerged from obscurity to become, within ten years, the uncrowned Head of State of England and Wales, Scotland and Ireland.

Key events

1628 Elected MP for Huntingdon

1629 Charles I dissolves Parliament. Start of 11-year period of rule without Parliament

1640 Elected MP for Cambridge. Member of Long Parliament

1641 News of Irish Rebellion reaches London (1 November)

1642 Charles I attempts to arrest the Five Members (4 January)
Start of the Civil War (22 August)

1643 Cromwell sent as colonel to Eastern Association army (January)

1644 Promoted Lieutenant-General in reorganised Eastern Association army under the Earl of Manchester (January–February)
Commands cavalry in defeat of Royalists at Battle of Marston Moor (2 July)
Supports Self-Denying Ordinance and creation of New Model Army. Exempted from Self-Denying Ordinance (December 1644–March 1645)

1645 Commands cavalry in defeat of Royalists at Battle of Naseby (10 June)

1646 End of Civil War (May)
Cromwell returns to Westminster (June)

1647 Scots hand Charles I over to English Parliament (January)
Cromwell leaves London to rejoin the army (3 June)
Army occupies London (6 August)
Cromwell negotiates with King on the *Heads of the Proposals* (August–October)
Takes part in the Putney Debates (28 October–8 November)

1648 Commands one of three Parliamentary armies in the Second Civil War (May–October)
Arrives in London after Pride's Purge (6 December)

1649 Member of the High Court at the trial of Charles I (January)
Crushes Leveller mutinies (May)
Campaigns in Ireland (August 1649–June 1650). Massacres at Drogheda and Wexford (September and October)

1650	Campaigns in Scotland (July 1650–August 1651). Battle of Dunbar (September)
1651	Defeats Royalists at Battle of Worcester (3 September)
1653	Dissolves the Rump Parliament (20 April)
	Opens the Nominated Assembly ('Barebone's Parliament') (4 July)
	Installed as Lord Protector under the *Instrument of Government* (16 December)
1654	Opens first Protectorate Parliament (4 September)
1655	Appoints Major-Generals (August)
1656	Opens second Protectorate Parliament (September)
1657	Accepts *Humble Petition and Advice* but refuses offer of the crown (May)
	Second installation as Lord Protector (26 June)
1658	Dissolves second Protectorate Parliament (4 February)
	Death of Oliver Cromwell (3 September)

Country gentleman and MP, 1628–42

MP for Huntingdon

In 1628, Oliver Cromwell, aged 29, entered public life for the first time when he was elected to be one of the two Members of Parliament (MP) for Huntingdon. This was the third Parliament summoned by Charles I and, like the previous two, it was soon at odds with him. Within three months the King had been forced to accept the Petition of Right and its demands that he should no longer imprison his subjects without trial or raise taxation without the consent of Parliament.

Many MPs also disagreed with the King about religion, believing that, with the help of Archbishop Laud, he intended to steer the Church of England away from its established Protestant position back towards beliefs and practices which they associated with Roman Catholicism. Cromwell was one of those who most feared this. Before the House of Commons could develop its protest Charles I dissolved Parliament and proceeded to rule without it for the next 11 years.

MP for Cambridge

In 1631, Cromwell sold most of his property in Huntingdon and moved with his wife and family to nearby St Ives. In 1636 his uncle died leaving him the house in Ely where his mother had been born, as well as other property in the town. Once again, the Cromwells moved.

Figure 1 Oliver Cromwell
painted by Robert Walker.
Cromwell was born in Huntingdon
in 1599. He was educated at
Huntingdon Grammar School and
then at Cambridge University where
he was a member of Sidney Sussex
College. He left after only a year, in
1617, following the death of his
father. In 1620, he married
Elizabeth Bourchier, the daughter of
a wealthy London merchant who
had also bought land in Essex. They
set up house in Huntingdon and
farmed the lands that Cromwell had
inherited from his father.

Figure 2 Elizabeth Bourchier,
Cromwell's wife by an unknown
artist. The Cromwells apparently
enjoyed a close and affectionate
marriage. 'My life is but half a life in
your absence', Elizabeth wrote to her
husband in 1650. They had eight
children: Robert, born in 1621, Oliver
(1623), Bridget (1624), Richard (1626),
Henry (1628), Elizabeth (1629), Mary
(1637), and Frances (1638).

In 1640, when Charles I eventually called another Parliament, Cromwell was invited to stand for election in the town of Cambridge. He sat as MP for Cambridge, first in the Short Parliament, which lasted only three weeks, and then in the Long Parliament which met at Westminster on 3 November 1640 and remained in session until 1653.

The Long Parliament

For several months members of the Long Parliament were united in their campaign to punish those who had helped the King to rule on his own for 11 years, and to dismantle the apparatus which had enabled him to do this. By late 1641 some MPs believed enough had been done to limit the King's powers; others, led by John Pym who was master-minding the opposition, wanted to go further. Pym and his allies did not trust Charles I and wanted to ensure that he could never reverse the changes to which he had reluctantly agreed. Cromwell belonged to this group. While he was probably not a leading figure in it (see Chapter 1), he was certainly an enthusiastic one, for he had returned to London in 1640 changed in one important way from 11 years pre-viously. Sometime between 1626 and 1638 he went through a deep religious experience which left him even more firmly committed to his Puritan beliefs. He was more determined than ever to protect what he believed to be Parliament's rights and freedoms, and to fight for a 'godly' church which would reform both people's spiritual lives and their day to day behaviour.

On 1 November 1641 news of an uprising of Catholics in Ireland played on Cromwell's worst fears. Like most Puritans, he was all too ready to believe the exaggerated reports of a horrific massacre of English Protestants. This, he thought, was only the prelude to a Catholic inva-sion of England: the Irish Rebellion had to be suppressed. An army had to be raised, but once raised it might be used by the King against Parliament itself. To avoid this, Pym proposed that in future the King's advisers should be approved by Parliament. For moderate MPs this was going too far but others, including Cromwell, believed the King capable of using force against his Parliamentary opponents. His fears were soon confirmed by Charles's botched attempt to arrest the Five Members. Cromwell urged his colleagues to prepare for a war and, before it had officially begun, he risked a charge of treason by leading a raid to seize gold, silver and money on its way to the King in York.

Soldier and politician, 1642–49

The Civil War, 1642–46

1 From Captain to Lieutenant-General

When the Civil War began Cromwell had had only a little experience as a politician and none as a soldier. Four years later he had become an important political figure and a highly respected cavalry commander. He started as a captain in the Earl of Essex's army and fought at the Battle of Edgehill. In 1643 he was promoted to Colonel and sent to East Anglia which Parliament had recently organised into a regional group known as the Eastern Association. There he energetically drummed up support for Parliament and organised the area's defence. In 1644 Parliament reorganised the Eastern Association army under the command of the Earl of Manchester. Cromwell was made second-in-command and promoted to Lieutenant-General. In June that year his cavalry played a decisive part in defeating the Royalists at the Battle of Marston Moor, and his military reputation soared.

2 Victory for the 'war group'

Cromwell then became involved in a quarrel with his commanding officer. Parliament was divided between a 'peace group' who were anxious to come to an agreement with the King as soon as possible and a 'war group' who wanted to ensure total victory over him. Manchester belonged to the first group, Cromwell to the second. In the House of Commons Cromwell accused Manchester of failing to prosecute the war with sufficient vigour. He then helped his allies in the Commons and Lords to push through the Self-Denying Ordinance in 1645 making it illegal for any MP to hold an army command. By this device the less determined generals were removed. Sir Thomas Fairfax was appointed commander-in-chief of the New Model Army, an amalgamation of Parliament's existing three armies.

Cromwell did not resign, probably because Parliament granted him a series of temporary exemptions. His enemies claimed he had planned this in advance. It is more probable that he took the risk of sacrificing his own command in order to remove those who lacked his zeal. Because his military skills made him indispensable, he was appointed Lieutenant-General of Horse and Fairfax's second-in-command. His cavalry then continued to play a central role in defeating the Royalists, notably at the battles of Naseby and Langport.

Parliament, army and King, 1646–49

At Westminster, June 1646–May 1647

When the Civil War ended, Cromwell's commission was not renewed and he returned to Westminster to continue as an MP. He wanted to ensure that any settlement with the defeated King, firstly, fully protected Parliament's freedoms and secondly, provided sufficient religious toleration to allow individual Protestant congregations the freedom to worship as they chose. He was, therefore, dismayed to find that a group of MPs known as Presbyterians now dominated Parliament. They supported the introduction of a Presbyterian National Church organisation, like the one in Scotland, and opposed any degree of toleration. Moreover, they appeared over-trustful of the King and planned not only to disband the army, but to do so without even paying the troops.

During the war Cromwell had recruited soldiers who believed in the cause for which they were fighting. He had forged close links with these men and believed that it was thanks to them that the Parliamentary cause had triumphed. Cromwell therefore tried to defend the army against the Presbyterians. At the same time he tried to reconcile the two sides since he believed the army should obey Parliament. Above all he wanted unity; but when Parliament finally voted to disband the New Model Army, it was clear he had failed. His next move was a turning point. He left Westminster and rejoined the army with his old rank as Lieutenant-General.

The army, June 1647–November 1647

The Army Council

Officers and soldiers in the army now organised themselves politically, creating a General Council of the Army to run their affairs. This consisted of officers and two soldiers from each regiment elected by the rank-and-file. These were known as 'Agitators'. The Army Council declared that the army would not disband until the soldiers had been paid and Parliament had taken account of their views on a settlement with the King.

The march on London

The army then marched towards London threatening to achieve its aims by force if it could not win them by persuasion. Cromwell, however, stayed in touch with his allies in Parliament, and continued to work both for an agreement between army and Parliament and for a settlement with the King. While sympathising with the soldiers, he tried to tone down the Agitators' more extreme demands in order to reassure the Presbyterians. He continued to hope that Parliament would make a settlement with the King which the army could support. He opposed the use of force to impose the army's demands on Parliament because it would be unconstitutional, and unpopular in a country sick of armies and war.

The occupation of London

When it became clear that the Presbyterians were prepared to ignore the army's demands altogether, Cromwell gave way. The army occupied London and expelled the hostile MPs. The Army Council had drawn up its suggestions for a settlement with the King in a document called the 'Heads of the Proposals'. Cromwell hoped that Parliament would now accept these so that it could be left to negotiate with Charles I without further military interference.

The Levellers

A fresh obstacle to a settlement then arose from within the army itself. New Agitators were elected who sympathised with a London group known as the Levellers. In 'The Agreement of the People' they produced alternative proposals for a settlement with the King demanding, for example, that the right to vote for MPs should be extended to more people. When the Army Council debated these proposals at Putney, Cromwell appealed for unity; but discussion soon revealed an unbridgeable gap between the conservative views of Cromwell and the majority of officers on one side, and the more radical demands of the Levellers on the other. With the army on the verge of disarray, the officers moved to reassert their authority. When Leveller sympathisers mutinied at Ware, in Hertfordshire, they had 11 arrested and one shot.

From the Second Civil War to the execution of the King, December 1647–January 1649

Although Charles I appeared to negotiate with Cromwell and his parliamentary allies over the *Heads of the Proposals*, and with Presbyterian MPs over their separate proposals, his only serious negotiations were with a third group: the Scots. In December 1647 he agreed to establish a Presbyterian Church in England in return for the Scots' help in fighting Parliament a second time. Four months later Cromwell was back in the field dealing with a Royalist uprising in South Wales. Then he marched north and decisively defeated the Scots at Preston. By November 1648 the Royalists had been crushed.

The Second Civil War hardened attitudes towards Charles I within the army and among MPs. Many now argued that he was untrustworthy, personally responsible for the further bloodshed, and an obstacle to peace. Led by Henry Ireton (see Picture Gallery on page 18), the Army Council called for the King to be put on trial. Cromwell, too, felt a deep anger towards those who had fought against Parliament a second time and believed that Parliament's victory showed that God was on its side. Even so, he did not yet support the idea of putting the King on trial. He remained in the north and did not return to London until after Pride's Purge when Colonel Pride, acting on orders from Ireton and the Army Council, forcibly removed from Parliament those Presbyterian MPs who still wished to negotiate with the King. About three weeks later Cromwell accepted that Charles I had to go. Once committed, he became a leading member of the group of 'regicides' who organised the show trial and execution of the King.

Lord General, 1649–53

Supporting the Commonwealth, January–August 1649

After the execution of Charles I, the Rump Parliament ruled England. It was known as the 'Rump' because it consisted of those non-Royalist MPs elected to the Long Parliament in 1640 who had survived the army's purges of 1647 and 1648. It appointed a Council of State to run the country on a day-to-day basis and declared England to be a Commonwealth, or Republic. Although the army clearly wielded the real power, the Army Council hoped to avoid interfering further in government. Cromwell now worked hard to persuade old allies, who had left politics because they opposed the execution of the King, to return and support the new régime. To achieve this, it was important that the army should not appear too radical in its views. When soldiers mutinied, protesting that the new government was unrepresentative, Fairfax and Cromwell crushed the uprising and had three of the ring-leaders shot.

Ireland and Scotland, August 1649–September 1651

In August 1649 Cromwell left England as commander of an army sent to deal with Royalists in Ireland. Eight months later, after a largely successful campaign, he returned to a hero's welcome. Posterity, however, has been more critical, for soldiers under Cromwell's direct command committed two massacres at Drogheda and Wexford. These, at least in part, Cromwell saw as revenge for the massacre of Protestants he believed the Catholic Irish had carried out in 1641.

Fairfax had resigned, so the Rump now appointed Cromwell as army commander-in-chief. In the summer of 1650 he marched into Scotland where Charles I's son, Charles Stuart, had arrived to raise support for his cause. His spectacular defeat of a superior Scottish force at Dunbar was followed a year later by final victory over the Royalists at Worcester. Cromwell was convinced that these battles had been won with divine help and signalled God's approval of the causes for which he had been fighting from the outset. With the fighting over at last, he looked to the Rump to create a Commonwealth worthy of all the blood shed over the previous nine years.

Dealing with the Rump, September 1651–April 1653

Despite Pride's Purge, members of the Rump Parliament were cautious in their outlook and by no means as radical as Cromwell and his soldiers might have wished. Cromwell wanted three main things from the Rump:

1 Religious reform: to establish toleration for all Protestant congregations and bring in measures to ensure godly behaviour among the people.

2 Law reform: to create cheaper, simpler and quicker legal procedures.

3 A constitutional settlement: the Rump was not to rule for ever. It

was to set up a permanent constitution which would both command support and safeguard the principles of Parliamentary freedom for which the Civil War had been fought.

Although the Rump governed quite efficiently, Cromwell and his officers felt increasingly dissatisfied with its record on religious and legal reform. Cromwell himself also strongly opposed its decision to go to war with the Dutch. Despite this, he once again tried to raise support for the government among his old allies and opposed harsh penalties against Royalists in the hope that they too might eventually be reconciled to the régime. He even talked of a constitutional settlement that might have 'somewhat of a monarchical power in it'. The Rump itself appeared, first, to want to hold on to power indefinitely, and then to be on the point of setting up elections for a new Parliament that could not be guaranteed to return MPs in broad agreement with the army's views. In March 1653 Cromwell prevented a move by army officers to dismiss the Rump. A month later he ordered his troops to drive the MPs from the House.

The Nominated Assembly, May–December 1653

Free elections for a new Parliament were out of the question since the majority of MPs returned would have been Royalist. For Cromwell, the old problems remained: how to demonstrate the virtues of the republic to the great majority of people who disliked it; and how to frame a constitution which would both enshrine the freedoms of Parliament and ensure that MPs were elected who would bring about godly reform.

His solution was to summon to London about 140 men approved for their godly qualities by the army's Council of Officers which had taken over the running of the country once the Rump was dissolved. These 'Saints' were to form an assembly which was to:

◢ carry out the long awaited religious and social reforms. These, Cromwell thought, would improve people's lives so much that they would, in themselves, convert opponents into supporters;
◢ set up a new, permanent, constitutional settlement.

Once installed, the Assembly, against Cromwell's wishes, proceeded to call itself a Parliament and to act as such. Praise-God Barebones, a

London leather-seller, was not a typical member, but nonetheles. caused it to be nicknamed the 'Barebone's Parliament'. Most member: were gentleman, many of them university educated. A very few were Fifth Monarchists who believed that Christ was about join his Saints to rule on earth for a thousand years, and that their duty was to prepare for this with radical reforms.

It was this minority which gave the Parliament a reputation for extremism which alienated the conservative country gentlemen Cromwell most wished to impress. However, many of the less eccentric majority also proved a disappointment, being hostile to religious toler ation, or to the army, or to both. With relief Cromwell accepted a paper signed by 80 of them handing their powers back to him.

Lord Protector, 1653–58

Healing and settling

Cromwell's priority now was to find a form of government acceptable to as many people as possible. What was needed, he thought, was a period of 'healing and settling'. In the hope of achieving this, he accepted a constitution drawn up by one of his generals, John Lambert (see Picture Gallery on page 19). The Instrument of Government established:

◢ a Protector, who had to govern with the help of:
◢ a Council of State, and
◢ a single chamber Parliament.

Cromwell was installed as Lord Protector for life and his successor was to be chosen by the Council. With his family, he moved into the old royal palace at Whitehall, from where he introduced measures to reform the law and improve the quality of church ministers. The Instrument itself provided for freedom of religious belief among Protestants and charged the Protector to guarantee this.

Once again Cromwell tried to encourage Royalists to support the new government; but when he called the first Protectorate Parliament it was clear how narrow his support had become even among those who had been his allies. Each time he had used the power of the army to inter vene in government he had made a new enemy. The election of 1654 returned many republican MPs angry at Cromwell's treatment of the Rump, and many others who believed the Instrument gave too little power to Parliament. Instead of passing laws Parliament debated the rights and wrongs of the new constitution. When Cromwell demanded that all MPs should sign a paper formally accepting the principle of government by a single person and a Parliament, about a hundred withdrew rather than do so. The remainder continued to criticise the Instrument causing Cromwell to dissolve Parliament at the earliest opportunity.

The Major-Generals

In 1655 there were several poorly organised Royalist uprisings, of which Penruddock's Rising in Wiltshire was the most significant. Although none posed a real military threat, Cromwell undoubtedly felt that his government was vulnerable. Aware of widespread opposition to his rule, he took the Royalist danger seriously. He divided the country into 11 districts and appointed an army Major-General to supervise each one. Significantly, the Major-Generals had two tasks:

- to suppress opposition to the government;
- to be responsible for the 'suppression of vice and encouragement of virtue': for the establishment, in other words, of godly rule.

The Major-Generals became widely unpopular. They were resented as military figures; as government agents interfering with the traditional role of local gentry in running local affairs; as suppressors (in the name of godly rule) of popular entertainments and customs; and as the collectors of a Decimation Tax on Royalists designed to pay for the Major-Generals themselves and new local militias. When Cromwell was forced to call another Parliament to vote money for a war with Spain, MPs refused to renew the Decimation Tax. Cromwell allowed the system of Major-Generals to fall into disuse.

Constable or King?

Many in Cromwell's Second Protectorate Parliament wanted to increase Parliament's role in government, reduce the Protector's powers, and set up a constitution which did not rely on the army. They also sensed that the majority of people in the country favoured a monarchy. As a result, in 1657, Parliament itself proposed a new constitution to Cromwell. The Humble Petition and Advice proposed government by a King, a Privy Council and a Parliament consisting of two houses. The lower house would have less powers than those allowed to it under the Instrument. Cromwell was invited to become the hereditary monarch.

Here was a proposal that might indeed provide Cromwell's longed-for settlement. It came from Parliament, not the army. It respected Parliamentary liberties. It reintroduced an upper house to provide some check on the lower. Cromwell's acceptance would at last win round the many country gentry who had opposed the government so solidly since 1649. Yet Cromwell could not bring himself to agree at once. For over a month he agonised. When his answer came it astounded MPs: he could not accept the title of King.

A few weeks later Cromwell was persuaded to accept instead an amended version of the Humble Petition and Advice in which he kept the title of Lord Protector. His motives were mixed and perhaps he was more comfortable with his view of himself as 'the good constable of the parish' rather than as King; but for many people Cromwell's refusal of the crown had poisoned the new constitution. It suggested that he was not, after all, prepared give up his reliance on the army, nor to abandon the unpopular mission he shared with his officers to introduce godly rule.

In the next session of Parliament his opponents were back in force. The republicans, with the backing of some army officers and various religious sects, again demanded an end to the Protectorate. Cromwell dissolved Parliament and dismissed the officers.

Six months later, he died. He had nominated his eldest surviving son, Richard, a civilian, to succeed him. Richard Cromwell was duly installed as Lord Protector. Within eight months, however, Richard had lost the support of his generals. He retired, leaving the country once more under the undisguised, and much resented, control of the army.

Twelve months later the country once again had the monarchy which most people desired. Oliver Cromwell's body was disinterred and hanged on the public gallows at Tyburn. His head was then severed from the body and stuck on a pole above Westminster Hall. His reputation had begun its long and controversial journey into history.

TASK

At A level you must develop the skill of taking useful notes from the books you read. Notes are important now because they give purpose to your reading and help you get into the topic. They will be important later as the basis of your revision before the exam.

You must be absolutely clear about which topics you want to make notes about, and make sure that you focus on those alone. Don't include material on other topics. Learn to leave out what you do not need.

Try this exercise. Read the section of Part One dealing with Cromwell's career between 1642 and 1646 (pages 8–9) and make notes on
◢ the key events which had an impact on Cromwell's career;
◢ his attitudes and beliefs.

Use one side of A4 paper only and set it out like this. Copy out the examples and then work through the section making your notes.

Cromwell's career 1642–46	
Key events	**Attitudes and beliefs**
1643 Parliament formed Eastern Association: Cromwell organised its defences.	
1644 Parliament reorganised the Eastern Association army: Cromwell made second-in-command.	*1644–45* Cromwell belonged to the 'war group' in Parliament. Believed Manchester was weak in his prosecution of the war.
1645 The Self-Denying Ordinance: Cromwell given exemption.	

You could now go on to make notes on the rest of Part One using the same topic headings. Or you could come up with your own headings.

Henry IRETON, *1611–1651*

During the Civil War Ireton fought as a Parliamentary cavalry commander, becoming a close friend of Cromwell who was attracted to his serious and thoughtful nature. In 1646 he married Cromwell's oldest daughter, Bridget. In 1647, like Cromwell, he left Westminster to rejoin the army and played a large part in drafting its manifestos. He was a main author of the *Heads of the Proposals* and a strong opponent of the Levellers. He led the demand for the trial of Charles I and was one of those who signed his death warrant. In 1650 he became second-in-command of the army sent to Ireland. He remained there as Deputy Lieutenant when Cromwell was recalled. His death the following year deprived Cromwell of one of his closest allies.

John LILBURNE, *c. 1614–1657*

He was a man of radical views whose initial admiration for Cromwell turned to outright hostility. In 1638 he was imprisoned for distributing unauthorised Puritan pamphlets. In 1640 Cromwell secured his release and in 1643 he used his influence to have Lilburne made an officer in Manchester's army. In 1646 Lilburne was imprisoned by the House of Lords for his criticism of Manchester. In 1647, as leader of the Leveller movement, he fell out with Cromwell whom he accused of betraying the cause of civil liberty and religious freedom. He claimed that Cromwell had appeared to support Leveller policies in order to unify the army, and then, that achieved, had turned on them in pursuit of his own personal power. In 1649 Lilburne bitterly attacked Cromwell for his part in the trial and execution of the King, and the Rump as an unrepresentative body. 'Free-born John' remained a thorn in the side of the régime until his death, suffering one period of exile and several spells in prison. In his final years he became a Quaker.

John LAMBERT, *1619–1683*

Starting as a cavalry commander in the Civil War, he proved an outstanding soldier. In 1647 he commanded the army in the north which defeated the Scots at Preston. In 1651 he achieved notable victories as Cromwell's second-in-command in Scotland. As a prominent member of the Council of Officers he devised and wrote the Instrument of Government. He became a member of the Council of State. He was a strong supporter of the Major-Generals scheme and was himself appointed to govern a large part of the north of England. Widely seen as Cromwell's most likely military successor as Protector, he opposed any reduction in the army's influence over government. In 1657 he stood out against the Humble Petition and Advice and, despite Cromwell's eventual rejection of the Kingship, refused to take the new oath of allegiance. When Cromwell forced him to resign his commission, he withdrew from both the army and politics. He returned after Cromwell's death and led the army in an unsuccessful attempt to prevent the restoration of Charles II. He was imprisoned for the rest of his life.

Roger Boyle, Lord BROGHILL, *1621–1679*

He was the younger son of the Protestant Earl of Cork and one of his brothers was the scientist Robert Boyle. During the Civil War he fought for the Royalists in Ireland. In 1649 Cromwell persuaded him to support the new Commonwealth. Broghill won over many other formerly Royalist Protestant families and persuaded Cromwell to treat them better. He admired Cromwell and became a close personal friend. In 1656, he was appointed President of the Council of State in Scotland where he managed to persuade important landowners to accept, even if not positively support, the rule of the Protectorate.

Back in London he worked for a civilian government based on the will of Parliament rather than on the power of the army. It was a severe blow to him when Cromwell refused the offer to become King made in the Humble Petition and Advice.

PART TWO

CHAPTER ONE

WHY DID CROMWELL OPPOSE THE KING?

Objectives

◢ To investigate Cromwell's background and his opinions on religious and political matters up to 1642

◢ To understand how and why historians' views about these have changed

◢ To explain why Cromwell opposed the King.

Key events

1616–17	Cromwell studies at Sydney Sussex College, Cambridge
1620	Marries Elizabeth Bourchier
1628	Elected MP for Huntingdon
1629	Charles I dissolves Parliament. Start of 11 years 'Personal Rule'
1630	Cromwell takes part in quarrel over Huntingdon town charter
1631	Sells property in Huntingdon and moves to St Ives
1636	Moves to Ely where he has inherited his uncle's house and property
1640	Elected MP for Cambridge in Short and Long Parliament
1640–42	Backbench MP in early sessions of the Long Parliament
	Long Parliament passes Acts to limit the King's powers (1640–41)
	The Commons begins to debate the Grand Remonstrance (November). News of Irish Rebellion reaches London
1642	Charles 1 attempts to arrest the Five Members and Lord Mandeville (January) Cromwell raises a troop of soldiers and ambushes a Royalist convoy outside Cambridge (August)

The invisible Cromwell

All biographers like to find out as much as possible about their subject's early years. They hope to come across important influences and experiences which may shed light on the actions, attitudes and beliefs of the older man or woman.

Biographers of Oliver Cromwell are no exception. Unfortunately, they run into trouble straight away because very little is known, not just about Cromwell's childhood, but about the first 40 years or so of his life. Here is a man who burst into prominence at the age of 43, and 13 years later became the only uncrowned Head of State that the countries of the British Isles have ever known. To do that he must have possessed exceptional qualities, and historians have tended to assume that these must have been somewhere in evidence before he became a public figure. But it is very hard to prove this because the sources relating to Cromwell's life before 1642 are so scarce. Through them we catch tantalising glimpses of the man but they provide no sustained view. We are dealing with nearly three-quarters of the lifespan one of the great figures of British history and yet there is hardly anything to go on.

Even so, historians have done their best to piece together a picture of Cromwell's life before 1642. In particular they have tried to answer those questions which may help us to understand how he rose to prominence during and after the Civil War:

◢ What was his social background?
◢ What were his political and religious opinions?
◢ Why did he oppose the King?
◢ What part did he play in the events leading up to the Civil War?

Until recently most twentieth-century historians have come up with similar answers to these questions, even if they hold different conclusions about Cromwell's career as a whole. In 1990, however, an article appeared which suggested that much of what historians had accepted as true about Cromwell's early life and background was either wrong or unprovable.

The traditional view

The traditional version of Cromwell's early career up to 1642 portrays him as a typical member of the group of MPs which led the opposition to Charles I in the 1640–42 sessions of the Long Parliament:

◢ a country **gentleman** used to local government;
◢ a man brought up to hold strict **Puritan** views;
◢ someone who believed strongly in Parliament's freedoms and who **opposed the King** locally during the 11 years of his personal rule;
◢ someone connected by **family** to key opposition figures and who

himself played a large part in planning and implementing opposition to the King.

KEY TERMS

Gentlemen formed the top rank of English rural society beneath the aristocracy with whom their families sometimes intermarried. They were landowners and lived off the profits of renting out their land to tenants. They were the leaders of their local society usually serving as Justices of the Peace and often as Members of Parliament. The gentry class was, however, a wide one. There was a big gap between those from wealthy and well-established gentry families, which might be better off than some of the nobility, and those with just enough wealth to put 'gent.' after their name.

Puritan is a term used by historians of the early seventeenth century to describe those members of the Church of England who called themselves 'godly'. The 'godly' believed that the Protestant reform of the Church, begun at the Reformation, should be carried much further. They were intensely hostile to any practice or ritual which so much as hinted at Roman Catholicism. They wanted to transform people's spiritual lives and also their social behaviour. For a fuller discussion, see page 29.

The main points usually put forward to support this picture o Cromwell's pre-1642 career are as follows:

1 Country gentleman

As Cromwell told Parliament in 1654 he was 'by birth a gentlemar living neither in considerable height nor yet in obscurity'. Althougl not one of the wealthiest, Cromwell was nevertheless a typical country gentleman whose family fortunes were founded on land acquirec when Henry VIII dissolved the monasteries. As such he would have played a significant role in local government, probably as a JP.

2 Puritan beliefs

Cromwell developed his Puritan views as a result of the teaching of hi schoolmaster in Huntingdon, Dr Thomas Beard, author of a Puritar book called *The Theatre of God's Judgements*. Later he spent a year at the strongly Puritan Sidney Sussex College in Cambridge. Sometim between 1626 and 1638 he went through a powerful religious experi ence which committed him still more firmly to the 'godly' cause.

3 Opposition to the King

A report of a speech which he made as an MP in the Parliament o

.628–29 shows Cromwell to have been a prominent opponent of the King's policies. On returning to Huntingdon he opposed the new Royal charter for the town. Its charter laid down how a town should be governed. Cromwell opposed the new one because it placed too much power in the hands of too few people. Meanwhile he was one of those who resisted Charles I's tax-raising efforts between 1628 and 1640 by refusing to buy a knighthood and opposing Ship Money.

4 'Lord of the Fens'

n 1638, Cromwell emerged as a defender of the rights of the common people against landowners who were draining the Fens in order to create farmland for growing food. This threatened the livelihood of poor people who had the right to graze animals on the common land which the drainers threatened to take over. Cromwell was reported as opposing the drainage scheme on behalf of the commoners, and thereby earned himself a reputation as 'Lord of the Fens'.

5 Family connections

One of Cromwell's aunts had married into the Hampdens, a well-known gentry family of Buckinghamshire. It was John Hampden who was famously prosecuted for his refusal to pay ship money. He was defended by Oliver St John who was married to one of Cromwell's cousins. Both Hampden and St John were to be leading opponents of the King in the Long Parliament.

Another aunt married into an Essex family, the Barringtons, which was connected to the Earl of Warwick. The Earl of Warwick was one of a group of Puritan aristocrats who was to lead the opposition to the King in the House of Lords. Cromwell's wife, Elizabeth, came from the Bourchier family, which was also linked to this group of influential Essex families.

6 Prominent backbencher, 1640–42

When he returned to London as an MP in 1640, Cromwell's family connections to key figures in the Parliamentary opposition to the King placed him at the heart of that opposition. Records suggest that, between 1640 and 1642, he played a central role in the attempt to put a permanent curb on the powers of the Crown.

Here is how Christopher Hill summarised this view of Cromwell in hi
biography, *God's Englishman*.

◢ Source

*Though himself a poor relation, he was connected both by birth and by his city
marriage with some of the most important families in the land, and with a group of men
who were organising opposition. He himself had played a part, in parliamentary
elections at Huntingdon, by his own participation in the 1628 Parliament and by his
battle against the corporation over the new town charter which imposed an oligarchy
on the town. He had been defeated by the power of the Royal government . . . . He had
also been in trouble with the government for his stubborn refusal either to take a
knighthood or to pay for not doing so, and surrendered only at the last possible
moment . . . . He opposed Ship Money. . . . In the dispute over Fen drainage he won
more than local notoriety as leader and organiser of the Commons' opposition. In this,
as in his attack on the Huntingdon oligarchy, he made himself the spokesman of
humbler and less articulate persons.*

*In all this we must recall his own position – member of the cadet (junior) branch of a
family which had risen to influence in the county on the spoil of the monasteries but
whose elder branch was declining. . . . His own economic position, however, was
moderately affluent after the death of Sir Thomas Steward in 1636. Oliver's hereditary
protestantism had been reinforced by his schoolmaster and friend Thomas Beard, by
his education at the very Puritan College of Sidney Sussex, by his own conversion, and
by reaction against the Catholicism fashionable at Charles I's court.*

*. . . his political connections and loyalties had been formed long before Parliament met
in 1640. When it did meet, he at once assumed a prominent role in its deliberation – not
in the very first rank, but far from the back benches. . . . He was the trusted colleague
of John Pym and John Hampden, the leaders of the Commons.*

Christopher Hill, ***God's Englishman*** (1971)

The re-assessment

Early career, 1599–1640

In 1990 the traditional view of Cromwell's career up to 1640 was
shaken by new research. 'Very little of this picture survives close
scrutiny', wrote John Morrill in *Oliver Cromwell and the English
Revolution* and he argued for a substantial revision of the picture:

Economic and social status

The evidence of subsidy rolls (tax assessments) suggests that Cromwell came from a more humble background than was previously thought. His inheritance from his father was not large. He was a gentleman; but a poor one. He was not a well-established country gentleman living in a manor off the income of his estates. He lived in town houses and had to work for his living. When he sold up in Huntingdon and moved to St Ives his income fell to the level of a *yeoman* rather than a gentleman. His inheritance from his uncle consisted not of the ownership of land but of the right to rent Church property belonging to Ely Cathedral and in return to receive the income from that land. This restored him to the gentry class, but only just.

KEY TERM

Yeomen formed the rank below the gentry. A yeoman could afford to rent sufficient land to qualify him to vote in Parliamentary elections, and he probably employed servants and labourers. But he was not wealthy enough to live and entertain in the style of a gentleman and probably had to do manual work himself. Prosperous yeomen aspired to be accepted as gentlemen and many were. There was considerable movement both up and down the social scale.

2 Experience of local government

There is no evidence that Cromwell ever held the most important job in local government, that of Justice of the Peace (JP) in the countryside. He was nominated as a JP for Huntingdon, but didn't take up the post. Even if he had done so, a town JP had far less responsibility than a rural one. There is no evidence, either, that he was a town councillor in Huntingdon, but it is probable that he was since he became its MP.

3 Puritanism

It is unlikely that Thomas Beard was responsible for teaching Puritan ideas to Cromwell, for there turns out to be no evidence that Beard was a Puritan. Historian John Morrill discovered that Beard was a pluralist – someone who held several Church jobs at once. He also combined his work as a priest with being a town councillor. Puritans believed that it was wrong to do both these things. In any case both Charles I and Archbishop Laud had dealings with Beard at various times and neither complained of Beard's Puritanism which they almost certainly would have done had he shown any leanings in that direction. As for Beard's

'Puritan' book *The Theatre of God's Judgements*, John Morrill argued tha
its ideas are those generally held by Protestants at the time rather tha
having an especially Puritan flavour. Finally, it is unlikely tha
Cromwell was brought up a Puritan because his father did not us
Puritan forms of words when he wrote his will. There is, however, n
doubt that by 1638 Cromwell had been through an important religiou
experience which made him one of the 'godly' and that this affecte
his attitudes very strongly (pages 28–29).

4 The 1628 Parliament

The theory that Cromwell played a significant part as a critic of th
government rests on a report of part of a speech he made in 1629. In i
he apparently complained about the way bishops were encouragin
the spread of **Arminian** ideas. John Morrill points out that othe
sources show the first part of the speech was not made by Cromwell a
all and that the second half referred to an incident that had taken plac
ten years earlier.

5 The Huntingdon Charter

John Morrill also shows that Cromwell had already been on the losin
side of an argument with the Corporation (town council). When th
new charter was agreed Cromwell was left off the list of aldermen, pe
haps as revenge. So Cromwell's complaint about the new charter wa
more likely to have been based on a grudge than on an issue of prin
ciple. The discovery of a sworn testimony by Thomas Beard tha
Cromwell had at first agreed with the new charter adds weight to thi
interpretation.

6 Opposition to Royal taxes

When Charles I ordered landowners with an income of £40 from thei
land to buy a knighthood, Cromwell was one of many who did not. I
1631 he was fined and eventually paid up. There is no evidence that h
held out for very long. He probably also paid Ship Money since he i
not listed as failing to do so.

7 'Lord of the Fens'

There is no evidence that Cromwell opposed fen drainage. As Protecto
he supported it and recalled that in the 1630s the rights of the com
mon people had not been sufficiently taken into account. It is mos
likely that Cromwell wanted to help them achieve compensatio

ather than that he opposed the scheme as a whole. Royalists invented he nickname 'Lord of the Fens' to draw attention to Cromwell's umble origins.

KEY TERM

Arminians were the followers of a Dutch theologian called Arminius whose ideas became popular in England in the 1620s and 1630s. Arminian doctrine rejected the Calvinist idea of predestination and stressed instead the importance of people's free will. It said that the sacraments of the Church, such as holy communion, were more important than preaching.

The Long Parliament, 1640–42

Historians have also cast doubt on the picture of Cromwell as a leading member of the opposition in the 1640–42 session of the Long Parliament.

Family connections

There is no doubt that Cromwell's family connections linked him with important figures in the opposition to the King. It is also probable that these links helped him to play a larger part in the affairs of the Long Parliament than he would otherwise have done given his lack of political experience. For example, he served on 18 Parliamentary committees; he moved the second reading of a bill for annual Parliaments which later became the Triennial Act; he was involved in the campaign to remove bishops from the Church of England which led in 1641 to the presentation to the Commons of the Root and Branch Bill; and he was prominent in moves to bring the militia under Parliamentary control.

But this does not mean that Cromwell was the close and trusted ally of Parliamentary leaders and a central opposition figure himself. As the historian, Barry Coward, points out in *Oliver Cromwell*, '. . . it is dangerous to assume at any time that family relationships are necessarily the basis for firm political alliances. Common sense suggests that love and affection are by no means the only type of relationship that exists between members of extended families.'

A central role?

So how central was Cromwell's role? Recently historians have stressed

that is unlikely that Cromwell was right at the heart of the oppositio
to the King because he was both hot-headed and prone to make quit
serious political misjudgments. On one occasion he was reprimande
for a verbal attack in the House on another MP; on another he got int
trouble with the chairman of a Common's Committee:

◢ Source

*… his whole carriage was so tempestuous, and his behaviour so insolent, that the
Chairman found himself obliged to reprehend him; and to tell him that if he proceeded
in the same manner, he would presently adjourn the Committee, and the next morning
complain to the House of him.*

From **The Life of Edward, Earl of Clarendon … By Himself** Volume 1 (182

On top of this, Cromwell's lack of judgement would have made him
dangerous ally: in John Morrill's words, 'an unguided missile not reall
under ground control'. Several of his speeches appear to have don
more harm than good to the causes he was supporting and he com
pletely misjudged the mood of the House when he asserted that 'ver
few would oppose the Grand Remonstrance'. The Remonstrance liste
the Commons' grievances against the King and demanded that i
future Parliament should appoint ministers. In fact many MPs di
oppose it and it was passed by a narrow majority of only 11 votes. Th
likelihood is that Cromwell was on the fringe of the group that master
minded the opposition to the King rather than at its centre.

The new picture that emerges of Cromwell's career up to 1642 is no
that of a man who steadily built up his experience of leadership firs
locally and then in Parliament. The reality was more complex
Cromwell's life involved many ups and downs and it appears that h
did not become a key figure in the opposition to the King until th
Civil War itself had begun.

Why did Cromwell oppose the King?

Religious beliefs

1 Cromwell's conversion

Sometime between 1626 and 1638 Cromwell went through an intens spiritual experience as a result of which he became a Puritan. It is impossible to say exactly when this happened, or how long it lasted, but it seems likely that the process was completed between 1629 and 1631. We know about it from a letter he wrote in 1638:

◢ Source

The Lord accepts me in His Son and gives me to walk in the light, as He is the light ... Blessed be his name for shining upon so dark a heart as mine! You know what my manner of life hath been. Oh, I lived in and loved darkness, and hated the light. I was a chief, the chief of sinners. This is true; I hated godliness, yet God had mercy on me. O the riches of His mercy!

W. C. Abbott (ed.), **The Writings and Speeches of Oliver Cromwell** Volume 1
(Cambridge, 1937)

The letter tells us that Cromwell now believed himself to be one of those whom Calvin called the Elect – people chosen by God to live an eternal life in heaven after their deaths. For this, like all Puritans, Cromwell would be for ever grateful and would give praise and thanks to God for saving someone so unworthy.

Cromwell calls himself the 'chief of sinners' and says he 'hated god-liness'; but this does not mean that previously he had led an immoral and unchristian life. These were simply the exaggerations which Puritans used when contrasting their old lives with their new. The point was that after what they regarded as their 'conversion' they lived at a level of religious awareness far higher than they had experienced before. They felt an intense personal relationship with God and were absolutely committed to leading a life of service to God. This involved seeking God's will through prayer and through reading and under-standing the Bible. They thought that most people merely went through the formal motions of religious observance. Because these people experienced no inner conviction, they failed to submit their lives to God's will.

2 The Puritan programme

By the end of James I's reign the majority of ministers in the Church of England accepted Calvin's teachings. In line with Calvinist thinking they dressed simply, not in robes, and believed in the importance of studying the Bible and preaching sermons. In these respects the Church of England had taken up a more extreme Protestant position than Elizabeth I had either wanted or expected when she introduced her Church Settlement. Puritans, however, felt that reform in the Church should be carried still further. They had two main aims in the 1630s: one essentially defensive; the other visionary.

The defensive aim was to purge the Church of England of any hint of Roman Catholicism. Although, by the 1620s, the Church was generally an extreme Protestant one, it continued to tolerate a broad range of opinion. Some of the ceremonies and practices associated with Roman Catholicism still survived. To Puritan eyes these were the work of Satan and had to be abolished. Roman Catholicism was the hated enemy against which the Church had to be defended at all costs.

The visionary aim involved nothing less than a transformation of social behaviour: the end of such things as drunkenness, swearing and sexual immorality. This 'reformation of manners' would in its turn lead people towards their own personal spiritual reformations. Social reformation would create the conditions for inner reformation and godliness.

These were the convictions to which Cromwell was committed by about 1631. When the Long Parliament assembled in 1642 they provided the driving force for his political actions.

Threats to Church and Parliament

Puritans were often important figures in their local communities. Some were aristocrats, many were gentry. They believed very strongly that people had the right to find God in their own way; but this was as long as they continued to accept their place in society. Puritans did not wish to disturb the social and political hierarchy. Nor, in the 1630s, were they campaigning to have their own Church. They were not separatists. They supported the idea of a national Church and saw themselves as part of the Church of England. Nor were they out to abolish bishops and change the way the Church of England was run.

It was the policies of Charles I which caused many of these attitudes to change. To Puritan eyes, the King appeared to be attacking two of the country's most central institutions: the Church of England and Parliament.

The threat to the Church

Arminianism

Charles I supported Laud's Arminian policies and appointed him as Archbishop of Canterbury in 1633. With its rejection of predestination and emphasis on sacraments, ceremony and ritual at the expense of sermons, Arminianism seemed to Puritans to be almost indistinguishable from Roman Catholicism. Laud's attempt to impose an Arminian form of service on every parish filled them with alarm and fury. Here was an attempt to pull the country back from the extreme Protestant position now accepted by the majority of English people. Far from being taken further, the Reformation was to be reversed.

Roman Catholicism

Equally seriously 'Popery' had penetrated the very heart of the court. The King was known to allow his French wife, Henrietta Maria, to hold Catholic masses. Some believed that there might be a conspiracy to overthrow the Church of England and substitute Roman Catholicism.

2 The threat to Parliament

Between 1629 and 1640 Charles I had ruled successfully without calling a Parliament. Using the Royal prerogative he had managed to find ways of raising taxes. Those who had resisted had been imprisoned. Meanwhile Archbishop Laud had used Church courts and the prerogative courts (which were outside Parliament's control) to force people to conform to his religious changes.

If the King could manage to rule without Parliament it meant the end of the tradition that he should take advice from the Lords and Commons and pursue policies which had their support. It was clear to men like Cromwell that Parliament had to be restored to what they saw as its rightful place in the process of government. It alone stood between the King's advisers and their apparent desire to reverse the Reformation.

Distrust of the King

Within a few months of the start of the Long Parliament its leaders achieved their aim of dismantling the apparatus of the King's personal rule. The King signed the death warrant of his minister, the Earl of Strafford and saw Archbishop Laud imprisoned in the Tower of London (where he was executed in 1645). He agreed to the abolition of prerogative courts such as Star Chamber and the Council of the North.

He accepted that in future it would be illegal to raise taxes withou Parliament's consent. He agreed to the Triennial Act stating tha Parliament should meet every three years.

It was in late 1641 that a so-far unanimous Parliament split betwee those who believed enough had been done to limit the King's powe and those who wished to go further. What caused Cromwell to sid with the latter?

1 Fear of military action

The crucial question was, could the King be trusted to keep to hi agreements? Cromwell was one of those who most feared that the Kin would take any opportunity to reverse Parliament's successes by threat ening or taking military action against it. He was particularly con cerned that the army used to defeat the Scots had not yet bee disbanded and by the revelation, in May 1641, of a plot to use it t overawe Parliament. The King wanted the plotters imprisoned to awai trial and opposed their release on bail. He also wanted the Earl of Esse to be given command of the militia on behalf of Parliament.

2 Fear of a Catholic conspiracy

The news of the rebellion of Irish Catholics in Ulster (page 98), whic arrived in London in November 1641 along with exaggerated report of appalling massacres of Protestants, stirred all Cromwell's fear He believed it marked the first step in a Catholic conspiracy to recon quer England. He was one of those most concerned to see the rebellio crushed. In 1642 when Parliament passed the Adventurers' Act whic raised money for troops to reconquer Ireland by promising subscriber that they would be repaid in land confiscated from the Catholic rebel Cromwell put up the substantial sum of £2,050. But he was equall concerned that any army raised to put down the rebellion might firs be used by the King against Parliament. Hence his support for Pym radical proposal that in future the King's advisers should be approve by Parliament.

'Violent spirits'

Charles I's attempt to seize the initiative by the arrest of the Fiv Members and Lord Mandeville made plain what Cromwell ha believed all along: the King was prepared to resort to force. Cromwe demanded that Parliament should take steps to protect the countr against the Catholic threat. He wanted Parliament to be able to levy forces that it, not the King, would control. Only in that way could the liberties of Parliament be protected. Parliament in turn would protect the Protestant Church and the hope of a godly reformation.

In March 1642 Parliament passed the Militia Ordinance to give itself the right to raise troops. By this time Cromwell was, in the words of a contemporary commentator, one of the 'violent spirits' in the Commons. In the coming months he called for measures to prevent supplies and equipment reaching the King. In August, before the official outbreak of war, he seized arms and ammunition in Cambridge Castle and intercepted valuables being sent under armed escort from Cambridge University to the King in York. Had Parliament's rebellion collapsed at that point he would have been open to charges of both theft and treason.

'That slovenly fellow'

As matters moved to a crisis in 1642 Cromwell appears to have become increasingly prominent within the Parliamentary opposition. His actions suggest a man whose hour had come. Until then the impression is of someone not completely at home in the political manoeuvrings at Westminster; a man of firm convictions, blunt speaking, and inclined to outbursts – someone of 'fiery' temper as his steward was later to describe him. Nor did he cut much of a figure in the House according to the Royalist, but reasonably fair, Sir Philip Warwick who recalled his 'plain cloth suit which seemed to have been made ill by a country tailor; his linen … not very clean, and … a speck or two of blood upon his little band, which was not much larger than his collar; his hat was without a hatband; his stature was of good size; his sword stuck close to his side; his countenance swollen and reddish; his voice sharp and untunable, and his eloquence full of fervour.'

Yet within this figure lurked exceptional qualities which some at least may have begun to notice. Years later in 1721, Sir Richard Bulstrode recalled some words John Hampden reportedly spoke to Lord Digby in 1642. Indicating Cromwell, he said, 'That slovenly fellow which you see before us, who hath no ornament in his speech; I say that sloven, if we should come to a breach with the King (which God forbid) in such case will be one of the greatest men of England'.

What Cromwell appears to have had, fuelled by his passionate reli
gious convictions, was the capacity to think the unthinkable and to g
where others feared to tread. While most MPs agonised over the right
and wrongs of making war on their sovereign, Cromwell was one o
those whose certainties led the way. His temperament suited him to b
a man of action, and in the crises of 1642 that is how he emerged.

As he rode with his hastily raised troop of 60 cavalry to join the Earl c
Essex and take part in the first battle of the Civil War at Edgehil
Cromwell was on the threshold of one of the most formative experi
ences of his life. An ingredient was about to be added to the making o
Oliver Cromwell which would transform both the man and his role ii
public affairs. That ingredient was the experience of war.

TASKS

How and why do historians' interpretations of the past change? You can
investigate this issue by looking at pages 21–28.

1 Identify all the points of difference between the old view of Cromwell's
early career and the new view put forward by John Morrill.

2 What evidence does John Morrill use to challenge the old view?

3 What kinds of questions do you think John Morrill asked about the old
view in order to uncover the new evidence?

4 Read Christopher Hill's summary of Cromwell's early career on page
24. Which of his statements are called into question by John Morrill's
work?

5 Write your own account of Cromwell's early career taking into account
Christopher Hill's summary and John Morrill's new evidence.

CHAPTER TWO

WHY DID CROMWELL DECIDE THAT THE KING SHOULD BE EXECUTED?

Objectives

◢ To understand Cromwell's attitudes to a peace settlement after the Civil War
◢ To understand his objectives in dealing with Parliament, the army and the King between 1646 and 1648
◢ To understand why he eventually came to the conclusion that the King had to be executed.

Key events

1646 Cromwell returns to Westminster (June)
1647 Scots hand Charles I over to English Parliament (January)
Cromwell is one of four Parliamentary representatives sent to the army at Saffron Walden (May)
Leaves London to rejoin the army (3 June)
Cornet Joyce seizes Charles I on behalf of the army (4 June)
Cromwell helps to draft the *Heads of the Proposals* and debates them in the Army Council at Reading (July)
The army occupies London (6 August)
Cromwell and his Parliamentary allies negotiate with King on the *Heads of the Proposals* (August–October)
The first *Agreement of the People* published (18 October)
Cromwell takes part in the Putney Debates (28 October–8 November)
Charles I escapes from Hampton Court and takes refuge on the Isle of Wight (11 November)
Cromwell helps to put down an army mutiny at Corkbush Field, Ware (15 November)
Charles I makes the *Engagement* with the Scots and rejects Parliament's peace proposals, the Four Bills (December)
1648 Cromwell supports Parliament's Vote of No Addresses (January)
Commands one of three Parliamentary armies in the Second Civil War (May–October)
Defeats the Scots at the Battle of Preston Pans
Remains in the North at the siege of Pontefract while the army calls for Parliament to be purged and the King to be put on trial (November)
Arrives in London after Pride's Purge (6 December)
1649 Member of the High Court at the trial of Charles I (January)

What were Cromwell's expectations after the Civil War?

The impact of the war

Cromwell's military experiences in the Civil War had a significan
impact on his attitudes and expectations once it was over.

1 His relationship with his soldiers

Cromwell formed a close relationship with both the officers and mer
under his command. He recruited 'men of spirit' who believed in the
cause for which they were fighting and who were also 'honest mer
such as fear God'. He imposed a strict discipline on them: it was saic
that 'no man swears but he pays his twelvepence . . .'. At the same time
he was concerned for their welfare. Consequently, at the end of the
war, Cromwell hoped that Parliament would look after the soldier
who had fought loyally on its side and brought it victory.

2 His religious views

In 1643, in return for the Scots' support in the war, Parliamen
promised to introduce a **Presbyterian** form of Church government ir
England similar to that of the Scottish National Church, or Kirk
Cromwell appears to have been happy to accept this, but he did no
support the idea of a National Church to which everyone had to
belong. He wanted some flexibility so that those who were obviously
'godly' could, if they wished, be free to worship in their own way. He
called this 'liberty to tender consciences'.

Presbyterian critics accused Cromwell and his fellow **Independents** o
encouraging the growth of religious sects. They feared that social orde
would break down if people were allowed to opt out of the Nationa
Church in order to worship in their own way. But Cromwell believec
that the army was setting an example to the country as a whole. Afte
the siege of Bristol he told the Speaker of the House of Commons
'Presbyterians, Independents, all had here the same spirit of faith and
prayer . . . they agree here . . . pity it is it should be otherwise any
where'. Whatever religious settlement was reached after the war, h
wanted it to include 'liberty of conscience'.

3 The experience of victory

As the war went on Cromwell became increasingly convinced tha

Parliament's victories were a sign that God was on its side and that the army was carrying out God's will: 'Sir', he wrote to the Speaker of the House of Commons after the Battle of Naseby, 'this is none other than the hand of God, and to him alone belongs the glory.' Since God had shown the justice of fighting the King, Cromwell wanted a peace settlement that fully secured all Parliament's objectives in going to war in the first place.

KEY TERMS

Presbyterians believed that it was against God's word to have a Church governed by bishops. They wanted one national Church to which everyone had to belong. Members of each parish would elect their own priest, or minister. Ministers and elected members of each congregation would meet in various assemblies to govern the Church's affairs.

Independents wanted each congregation to be free to worship as it chose, as long as it followed Protestant beliefs.

Divisions in Parliament

When Cromwell returned to Westminster in 1646 he found Parliament divided over how to use its victory over the King. At the time the two opposing groups of MPs were named after their two main religious groupings: Presbyterians and Independents. However, some historians today refer to them as the Political Presbyterians and the Political Independents because not every member of each political group was committed to the beliefs of the equivalent religious group:

1 The Political Presbyterians wanted the country to return to normal as soon as possible. In particular they:
   ◢ expected the King to accept the reductions in his powers made before the war;
   ◢ wanted him to agree to the introduction of a Presbyterian National Church organisation like the one in Scotland;
   ◢ wanted to disband the army. They thought this would make it easier to reach an agreement with the King. Also people were tired of paying for the upkeep of an army and having to provide soldiers in their area with free food and lodging.

2 The Political Independents distrusted Charles I and wanted stricter limits placed on him before he was allowed to return to London.

They also wanted to:

◢ maintain an army until the King agreed to terms;

◢ ensure that the new Church settlement would allow individual congregations the right to worship how they pleased.

Hopes for the peace settlement

Cromwell was both a religious and a Political Independent. His own aims were to ensure that:

◢ Parliament's freedoms were protected;

◢ there should be sufficient religious toleration to allow Independent congregations to flourish and thus eventually bring about the change in people's attitudes and behaviour which he called a 'godly Reformation'.

Parliament versus the army

Cromwell was dismayed to find that the Political Presbyterians dominated Parliament. They were particularly hostile to the New Model Army because they believed that, as a result of the encouragement of officers like Cromwell, it was full of Independents and members of other sects whose demand to worship as they pleased made them a danger to social discipline. They were talking not only of disbanding the army, but of doing so without even paying the troops any of the money they were owed. In March 1647 Parliament voted that it was illegal for the army to send any further petitions about its grievances.

1 Cromwell's aims

Cromwell's response was both to defend the army against this sort of treatment and to try to reconcile the two sides. Above all he wanted:

◢ unity between Parliament and the army. After all they were two vital parts of the same cause;

◢ an army obedient to Parliament. He believed that the army existed only because Parliament had ordered it to be created in the first place. Parliament held legitimate political authority which the army did not. Therefore the army should obey Parliament.

2 A widening split

Parliament's treatment of the New Model Army angered both officers and soldiers and hastened the process whereby a military organisation was turning itself into a political one. The rank-and-file in each regiment elected representatives, known as Agitators, to give their views to the Council of Officers which advised Fairfax, the commander-in-chief, and helped to make policy. The army's main demands were that before it was disbanded all soldiers should:

◢ receive a substantial amount of their arrears (backpay) in cash and a promise to pay the rest in due course;

◢ be granted immunity from prosecution for any actions carried out in the war. For example, soldiers wanted to avoid being taken to court for stealing a civilian's horse when in fact they had been ordered to commandeer it for use in a battle. Cases of this kind were becoming common now that the law courts were beginning to function again after the war.

3 Crisis

When, in May 1647, Cromwell and three other officer-MPs visited the army at Saffron Walden to attempt to reassure it on Parliament's behalf, they found it seething with discontent. Cromwell reminded the officers that they had fought to maintain the rights of Parliament and urged them to remain obedient for 'if that authority (Parliament) falls to nothing: nothing can follow but confusion'.

It was clear that officers were in control; but it was equally clear that the mood of the whole army was such that it would obey an order to disband only if it was treated fairly at the same time. Parliament's response was to order the army to disband without reference to any of the soldiers' demands or to any of the promises Parliament had already made. Officers and men immediately refused to obey. Cromwell's hopes of reconciling the two sides lay in shreds.

Why did Cromwell rejoin the army?

Faced with a direct confrontation between Parliament and army, Cromwell left London on 3 June 1647 and rejoined the army. If he believed that Parliament was the legitimate authority in the country, why did he abandon it and risk being portrayed as someone willing to threaten it with force?

1 A plot?

The day Cromwell arrived at the army's headquarters at Newmarket, a junior officer, named Joyce, led a troop of horses to seize Charles I who was being held by Parliament at Holmby House in Nottinghamshire. Joyce removed the King from Parliament's supervision and placed him under the control of the army. Cromwell's enemies claimed that he had organised this coup and that he had been deliberately encouraging the discontent within the army in order to turn it against Parliament: it was all a plot to enable Cromwell to take control of the army and gain his political objectives by threat of force.

Few modern historians accept this version of events. They believe Cromwell was genuinely working to reconcile Parliament and the army. It is true that, on his way to Holmby, Joyce visited Cromwell in London and that Cromwell therefore knew about Joyce's plans. But it is likely that it was the Agitators rather than the officers who had decided to seize the King and that Cromwell was simply being asked to approve their project.

2 Keeping control

Parliament's decision to disband the army probably convinced Cromwell that, as a known supporter of the army, it would be impossible for him to remain at Westminster for much longer. There are signs that he was preparing to leave. On 28 May, for instance, he collected arrears of army pay to which he was entitled. Perhaps Joyce's expedition decided Cromwell's timing for him. Once it was known that the King had been seized by the army, Cromwell was bound to be accused of plotting the King's capture and might face arrest if he stayed in London.

In addition, while Parliament was the legitimate authority in the land, the army was undoubtedly the most powerful. If the Agitators were behind Joyce's seizure of the King, it suggested that the army revolt was developing fast and that the officers might be about to lose control of it. Cromwell was probably alarmed and wished to use his authority to help the officers regain control. His aim was still to bring Parliament and army back together and he may have calculated that now he could best achieve this from within an army in which he had direct influence.

Parliament, Army and King, 1647–48

Cromwell's strategy

It appears that from his new base with the army Cromwell continued to pursue his old objectives of unity between Parliament and the army, and a settlement with the King which would achieve the aims of both religious and Political Independents.

The key elements in his strategy were:

- liaison with Parliament
- reassurances that plans for a peace settlement would not be too radical
- restraint of army extremists.

1 Liaison with Parliamentary allies

Cromwell kept in close touch with his Independent allies in both Houses of Parliament. He had worked with them during the Civil War, often relying on them to look after his interests when he was away fighting. Now, while he handled matters in the army, they promoted the Independent's aims in Parliament.

2 Reassurances

In various declarations the army did its best to reassure both Royalists and Presbyterians that its plans for a peace settlement were not too radical. It stressed that it was aiming at a peace settlement which was based on:

- the monarchy – the rights of the Crown should be considered as well as the rights of Parliament;
- a Presbyterian Church – the army went out of its way to explain that it could support this as long as there was provision for 'tender consciences'. Such provision, it said, should be extended to those who behaved 'soberly towards others' and 'peaceably towards the state'. In other words it was not, as some feared, to be a recipe for social disorder.

3 Restraint of army extremists

In discussions with the Agitators in the newly created Army Council Cromwell consistently tried to restrain those who argued for the army to use force against Parliament in order to get its way. 'Whatsoever you get by a Treaty', he said, '... it will be firm and durable ... that which you have by force, I look upon it as nothing.' He said he was agreeable to the use of the threat of force and if that failed there would be grounds for using force itself; but it was much better to proceed gradually since what was gained 'in a free way' was worth twice what was gained by force. When someone suggested that if the army used force once it would not be necessary again, Cromwell dismissed it as an 'anarchic proposal'.

4 Negotiation with the King

Meanwhile Cromwell and his fellow officers kept in close touch with the King. With their Independent allies in Parliament, they drew up the *Heads of the Proposals* which they hoped could form the basis of a treaty with him.

The Heads of the Proposals

This summarised Cromwell's aims for a peace settlement.

The Constitution

The King was to be restored to a 'condition of safety, honour and freedom in this nation' provided that he agreed:

- to call a parliament every two years;
- to a redistribution of Parliamentary seats in order to provide a fairer representation than before where there had been changes in population and wealth;
- that, for the next ten years, Parliament should control the army and navy and appoint the great officers of state.

Religion

- Bishops and clergy were no longer to have any civil authority over people's lives;
- It was no longer to be compulsory to attend church or to use of the Book of Common Prayer;
- No one was to be made to take the Covenant (the agreement to introduce a Presbyterian Church in England).

The war

An Act of Oblivion was to absolve all but a few Royalists from 'all trespasses, misdemeanours, etc. done in prosecution of the war'.

> **Reforms**
> Parliament was to attend quickly to 'things tending to the welfare, ease and just satisfaction of the kingdom' especially matters such as the reform of the law, in order to make it cheaper and quicker, and the system of maintaining priests by the paying of tithes.

The Leveller threat

Cromwell and the officers soon found themselves defending their position within the army itself. Many in the rank-and-file of the army had become influenced by the ideas of a civilian group in London calling themselves Levellers (see Chapter 3). The Levellers feared the Heads of Proposals would simply restore the old régime without addressing their concerns for radical reforms. In October 1647 newly elected Agitators drew up their own proposals, the *Agreement of the People* (page 52). It was discussed at a specially convened meeting of the Army Council held in Putney.

The Putney Debates

At Putney Cromwell's chief concern was to maintain the unity of the army. He therefore hoped to find common ground between the *Heads of the Proposals* and the *Agreement of the People*; but there was little to be discovered. The Putney Debates reveal Cromwell sticking to the line he had been taking for the past six months:

◢ the army should acknowledge Parliament's authority: 'Either they are a parliament or no parliament. If they be no parliament, they are nothing – and we are nothing likewise.';

◢ the peace settlement should centre on the restoration of the King's powers but with Parliament's role in the constitution guaranteed. Cromwell utterly rejected one officer's suggestion that the King should be prosecuted.

Discipline restored

In the event the unity of the army was restored not by the Putney Debates, which revealed deep splits between the Agitators and the majority of the officers, but by the officers' swift action on 15 November in crushing a Leveller revolt at Corkbush Field, near Ware. Cromwell may have been personally responsible for this; if not, he certainly approved. The sudden collapse of the Levellers suggests that support for them may not have run that deep; but another factor also played a part. On 11 November the King escaped from his army guards at Hampton Court and took refuge at Carisbrooke Castle on the Isle of Wight. The King's escape shocked the army and emphasised the need for unity within it. It was so helpful to Cromwell that his enemies accused him of plotting it himself. The evidence is unclear, but the probability is that he did not.

The Vote of No Addresses

Before his escape the King had two sets of peace proposals before him: a revised version of Parliament's 1646 proposals, the Propositions of Newcastle; and the Heads of Proposals recently offered by the army. Hoping to play Parliament and the army off against one another, the King had already indicated a preference for the Heads of Proposals. From the Isle of Wight he proceeded to reject Parliament's Four Bills which contained the main items from the *Heads of the Proposals* and to sign the *Engagement* (pages 111–12) with the Scots. Cromwell then supported Parliament's Vote of No Addresses which broke off negotiations with the King. He may have made a further attempt to win the King over. If he did, it failed. In May 1648, the Scots invaded England in an attempt to restore the King and the Second Civil War began.

By the end of December that year Cromwell had decided to support a purge of Parliament and the trial and execution of the King. Apparently he had reversed his opinion both about the use of force against Parliament and about the central importance of the King to any settlement.

Why did Cromwell change his mind?

The impact of the Second Civil War

1 The experience of war

As in the First Civil War the experience of military campaigning made a big impact on Cromwell. At heart he was a man of action and he found active campaigning exhilarating. Seen from the battlefield, rather from Westminster, political issues appeared simpler and clearer to him. Once again he experienced the comradeship of war and felt a renewed loyalty to the ordinary soldiers who fought for Parliament. He was also influenced by being close to the many officers and men who wanted religious and social reforms and who looked to him to represent their views. Consequently, he returned from the war with a renewed commitment to these causes. In short, the war further hardened Cromwell's belief that a settlement had to be reached which met the army's objectives.

2 Providence and the Saints

Like many other Puritans Cromwell believed in Providence: that is, that God directed human affairs. The signs of what God's will actually was could, therefore, be seen in daily events which were instances of God's intervention in human affairs, or 'providences'. Cromwell was convinced that his military victories in the Second Civil War, just as in the First, were 'providences' which confirmed that God supported the Parliamentary army and the cause for which it fought. The signs are, also, that from this time Cromwell started to go further and to believe that:

▲ because so many godly people, or Saints as they were becoming known, were in the army, the army represented the Saints-in-arms;
▲ because the Saints-in-arms had been so successful in battle, God had given the army a special part to play in putting His will into practice.

3 A supreme power?

As a result of his ideas about the role of the army Cromwell began to modify the way he thought about Parliament as the supreme power. If the army had a God-given mission it was possible to argue:

▲ that the army, not Parliament, was the true custodian of the cause for which two civil wars had been fought;
▲ that the army had become a legitimate political power in its own right.

'This army', Cromwell suggested to his friend Robert Hammond on 25 November 1648, was a 'lawful power, called by God to oppose and fight against the King upon some stated grounds'.

Although still reluctant to see force used against Parliament, there is no doubt that by the time of Pride's Purge Cromwell had persuaded himself that the army's duty of obedience had become conditional on

Parliament's attitudes. In his letter to Hammond he accused Parliament of 'Malice, swollen malice against God's people, now called "Saints"' and he argued that since God had called the army into 'power' for a purpose it had the right to oppose Parliament in order to achieve that purpose.

'In a waiting posture'

It is important, however, to remember that it was not Cromwell but other army officers, led by Henry Ireton, who masterminded Pride's Purge. Cromwell was on his way south from Pontefract and had responded very slowly to an order from Fairfax to return to London, making sure that he arrived after the purge. On 25 November he had told Hammond that 'we in this Northern army' had been 'in a waiting posture, desiring to see what the Lord would lead us to'. It appears that although he knew the matter was being discussed by senior officers, Cromwell did not want to take the lead in purging Parliament.

As so often in his career when a critical moment was reached, Cromwell hung back trying to work out what God wanted him to do. The pattern was to be repeated several times in the future. First Cromwell would withdraw for a time. Other people would then take initiatives which moved the situation on. Then, suddenly, Cromwell would decide on his course of action, re-enter the fray and re-establish his control of affairs. In doing this he displayed a mixture of genuine heart-searching and clever political calculation which makes it hard for the historian to disentangle his motives.

In the case of Pride's Purge, for example, he manage to distance himself from the use of force against Parliament and then to approve it immediately afterwards. It is likely that, quite apart from having some genuine doubts as to whether or not the use of force would be for the best, he was also glad to avoid direct responsibility for the purge since it left him free to continue the search for a last-minute settlement with the King.

'That man of blood'

The Second Civil War caused Cromwell to harden his attitude towards all those who fought against Parliament a second time.

◢ Source

Their fault who hath appeared in this summer's business is certainly double to theirs that were in the first [i.e. the First Civil War], because it is the repetition of the same offence against all the witnesses that God has borne, by making and abetting to a second war.

Oliver Cromwell writing in 1648. Quoted in W. C. Abbott (ed.),
The Writings and Speeches of Oliver Cromwell Volume 1 (Cambridge, 1937)

Cromwell called for severe penalties against their leaders and by the end of the year he had included the King himself among those who should be punished.

After Pride's Purge it was Ireton again, rather than Cromwell, who drove forward plans to bring the King to trial. Cromwell continued to see if any agreement could be reached with the King. As it became clear that Charles I was still not serious about negotiations, Cromwell's attitude hardened further. The King was a double-dealer who had plunged the country back into bloodshed as a result of his Engagement with the Scots. He had chosen to wage war on his own people despite the fact that, as Cromwell saw it, God had already passed judgement against him by giving Parliament victory in the First Civil War. He was, in short, a 'man of blood'. Cromwell gave up and joined the regicides telling the House of Commons at the end of December 1648 that 'Providence and necessity' dictated that the King should be brought to trial and executed.

'Willing to part with all'

By 'necessity' Cromwell meant that there was no choice left other than to execute the King because he had proved incapable of honest negotiation. But what is necessary, of course, always depends on your point of view. What Cromwell saw as 'necessity', others, including many of his recent allies, saw differently. Many Political Independents had already withdrawn from Parliament because they disapproved of Pride's Purge. They wanted nothing to do with the regicide either.

The fact is, Cromwell did have a choice in December 1648. He too could have withdrawn from public affairs in the face of the enormity of the prospect of executing the King. He chose to go ahead because of his religious beliefs and, as often happened once he had made a decision, he now pursued his objective with passion and conviction. 'We will cut off his [the King's] head with the crown on it' he reportedly told someone who questioned the legality of bringing the King to trial.

Yet for all his conviction the signs are that Cromwell did not act in a completely blinkered way. He was aware of how bold a step he and the other regicides were taking and he could see that it was conceivable that they were mistaken. For it was always possible that he might have misread God's will. When he wrote to Robert Hammond before Pride's Purge he wanted to persuade Hammond to commit himself to support for the army's actions rather than to stand on the sidelines. In urging Hammond to 'act' he admitted that the danger in committing oneself to an action was that it might be the wrong one. The person acting wrongly might one day suffer for it. But it was a risk that had to be taken: 'Who acts and resolves not through the Lord to be willing to part with all?'

A year after the execution of Charles I he was to write something similar to his old ally Lord Wharton who had also withdrawn in protest at Pride's Purge and the regicide. He assured Wharton that 'we are not triumphing' and then went on, 'We may (for aught flesh knows) suffer after all this. The Lord prepare us for his good pleasure!'

In December 1648 Cromwell took a decisive and momentous action and joined the small group which masterminded the trial and execution of the King; but he was aware that if he had misread God's will in the matter, he in turn stood to be punished. In the coming years he would seek earnestly for signs that God did in fact approve of what he had done.

TASKS

This chapter has dealt with one of the key questions which historians try to answer about Oliver Cromwell: why did he eventually decide to support the trial and execution of Charles I? Here is an exercise to help you use the chapter to reach your own answer to that question.

1 The influence of events

Identify the key events which took place between January 1647 and January 1649. Make a two-column chart headed 'Event' and 'Cromwell's response'. In the Event column note the events in order and, opposite, in the Response column make a note of Cromwell's reaction to each one. For example:

Event	Cromwell's response
Parliament made it illegal for the army to petition about its grievances.	Cromwell tried to reconcile Parliament and the army.

2 The options open to Cromwell

Identify each of the key decisions made by Cromwell in the same period. For each one say:

a what you think were the various choices open to him;
b why you think he made the choice he did.

Start with Cromwell's decision to rejoin the army in June 1647.

3 The role of the King

Prepare and write an essay in answer to the question 'To what extent was Charles I's failure to compromise the main cause of Cromwell's decision to support the trial and execution of the King?'

Remember that this is a 'to what extent' question. That means you must consider the influence of other factors and suggest how important you think they all were.

CHAPTER THREE

WAS CROMWELL A SOCIAL AND POLITICAL CONSERVATIVE? OLIVER CROMWELL AND THE LEVELLER MOVEMENT 1647–49

Objectives

◢ To examine Cromwell's motives and actions in his dealings with the Levellers

◢ To interpret and evaluate contemporary source material and reach conclusions about Cromwell's motives and intentions.

In the autumn of 1647 and the summer of 1649 Cromwell acted decisively to stem the development of further radicalism and support for the Levellers in the army. How much of a social and political conservative was Cromwell? This question can only be answered fully by an appraisal of his actions throughout the period of his influence and power, but his dealings with the Leveller movements provide an insight into his attitude to proposals for radical reform. An emphasis on the need to avoid measures which would provoke dissension and disunity is evident throughout his responses. The question still remains for us to consider how far practicalities and constraints were an excuse used to mask resistance to more radical reforms and how far they were genuine. This case study gives you the opportunity to consider these issues, using the evidence of Cromwell's speeches and writings: the evidence of his critics writing at the time and views of historians. The sources in this case study need to be studied in the context of the framework of events given in Chapters 2 and 4.

Key events

1647   *Regal Tyranny Discovered* is published by John Lilburne (currently imprisoned by the House of Lords). This was both an attack on the concept of monarch and on Charles I (January)

The *Large Petition* presented to the House of Commons (March) – containing requests for a range of social and political reforms

A New-found Stratagem published by Overton – an open appeal to the army for support (April)

The Large Petition condemned by the conservative majority in the Commons (May). Ordered to be burnt by the common hangman

Leveller influence evident in the army

The Case of the Armie Truly Stated is published (15 October) and presented to the Army Council. This Leveller–Agitator paper combined army grievances with the Leveller proposals for constitutional reform.

Cromwell takes part in the Putney Debates (28 October–8 November). The Leveller draft constitution, the *Agreement of the People*, discussed.

Cromwell helps to put down the army mutiny at Ware (15 November). The Levellers lose the prospect of military action in support of their programme and are virtually powerless

1648 Levellers return to tactic of petitioning Parliament (January). *Earnest Petition*, presented but to no effect

Levellers control the *Moderate*, a weekly newspaper, as a vehicle for their view (June–September 1649)

Assassination of Rainsborough, an influential pro-Leveller army officer, provokes huge demonstration at his funeral in London (29 October).

With the prospect of a treaty between Charles I and the 'Presbyterians' in Parliament, Cromwell and Ireton decide to look again to Levellers for support. Negotiations reopened

A series of meetings between army leaders and Leveller leaders to negotiate a common programme of reform (November)

The Whitehall debates held. Representatives of army leaders, Levellers, and political and religious Independents begin working on a new *Agreement of the People* (December–January 1649).

Disagreements, particularly over religious toleration, lead to the publication of two separate agreements

Levellers' *Second Agreement* published (14 December). This is more moderate than the first and allowed some restrictions to the Franchise

1649 The *Officers Agreement* presented to Parliament in the form of a petition. Rejected (20 January). Execution of the King effectively leaves the country in the control of a new set of rulers backed by military force

Levellers begin attacks on Grandees, using tactic of army subversion and popular demonstrations

Leveller petitions circulate in the army. Trial of Charles I attacked as illegal (February)

Lilburne presents *England's New Chains Discovered* (Part 1) to Parliament (26 February)

Overton publishes *Hunting of the Foxes ... Or Grand Deceivers Unmasked*
(21 March). This was not only a scathing attack on Cromwell and Ireton, it was
also a call to the army to mutiny against the new republic
England's New Chains Discovered part 2 published
Leveller leaders including Lilburne and Overton arrested on the orders of the
Council of State and confined in the Tower (28 March).
Levellers third and most radical *Agreement* published (1 May)
Army mutinies. About 1200 soldiers are surprised and overwhelmed at Burford on
14 May by a force from London led by Fairfax and Cromwell
Publications and petitions to Parliament continue, but Levellers have been
defeated as a political movement (May–September).

What did the Levellers want?

The *Agreement of the People*, published on 3 November 1647, can be
seen as the Levellers' proposed constitution for England. It was this
document that was debated a few days earlier at Putney. They demanded:

1 Parliamentary reform

◢ A single chamber – not a separate House of Commons and House
of Lords;
◢ Biennial Parliaments – elections to be held every two years;
◢ Redistribution of seats – so that the size of constituencies
correspond more nearly to their voting population.

2 Reform of the Franchise

The proposals of the *Agreement* of 1647 implied a virtually universal
suffrage; the vote was to be given to all those who were prepared to
sign the agreement. In addition to the considerable changes proposed
in these reforms, there were two aspects of the *Agreement* which represented something very new in English constitutional history:

◢ the idea of the written constitution and one which all who wished
to take part in political life would have to sign up to;
◢ the concept of **reserved powers**; that is, powers which belonged to
the people alone and which no government could give to itself.

KEY TERM

Reserved powers would not allow any government to:
◢ introduce conscription to the army;
◢ deny individual equality before the law or religious toleration.
Underpinning the concept of reserved powers was the concept that the people
were sovereign. Governments had the powers they had by consent of the
people. Some rights were so fundamental to individual liberty that
governments were not allowed to exercise them.

How did Cromwell react to the Leveller programme?

1 What Cromwell said

The Putney Debates were recorded fully by William Clarke, Secretary to
the Army Council who took down Cromwell's words in his own version
of shorthand writing (Source 1).

◢ **Source 1**

*These things that you have now offered they are new to us: they are things that we
have not at all (at least in this method and thus circumstantially) had any opportunity to
consider because they came to us but thus as you see; this is the first time we had a
view of them.*

*Truly this paper does contain in it very great alterations of the very government of the
kingdom.*

*And what the consequences of such an alteration as this would be if there were
nothing else to be considered, wise men and godly men ought to consider. If we could
leap out of one condition into another, I suppose there would not be much dispute –
though perhaps some of these things may be very well disputed. How do we know if
whilst we are disputing these things another company of men shall [not] gather
together and put out a paper as plausible perhaps as this? ... And not only another,
and another, but many of this kind. And if so, what do you think the consequence of
that would be? ... Would it not be utter confusion?*

*And if so what would that produce but an absolute desolation – an absolute desolation
to the nation and we in the meantime tell the nation 'It is for your liberty 'tis for your*

privilege; 'tis for your good'. But truly I think we are not only to consider the probability of the ways and means to accomplish [the thing proposed]: that is to say whether according to reason and judgement the spirits and temper of the people of this nation are prepared to receive and to go on along with it.

IV

Give me leave to say this. There will be very great mountains in the way of this and, therefore, we ought to consider the consequences. It is not enough to propose things that are good in the end. It is our duty as Christians and men to consider consequences and to consider the ways. ... I say it to you again, and I profess unto you, I shall offer nothing to you but that I think in my heart and conscience tends to the uniting of us.

V

It is not enough for us to insist upon good things that every one would do. There is not [one in] forty of us but could prescribe many things exceeding plausible – and hardly anything worse than our present condition, with all the troubles that are upon us. It is not enough for us to propose good things, but it behoves honest men to see whether, taking all things into consideration, they may honestly endeavour and attempt that proposed.

VI

But [first of all there is the question what obligations lie upon us and how far we are engaged]. If I be not much mistaken, we have in the time of our danger issued out declarations; we have been required by the Parliament ... to declare particularly what we meant. And therefore having heard this paper read, this remains to us: that we again review what we have engaged in, and what we have that lies upon us. And therefore I have no more to say but this: we having received your paper, we shall amongst ourselves consider what to do: and before we take this into consideration, it is fit for us to consider how far we are obliged, and how far we are free.

Extracts from Cromwell's response to the **Agreement**, 29 October 1847
The paragraph numbering is ours, not William Clarke's

1 Study paragraphs I and II. In what ways is it evident from these paragraphs that Cromwell was taken aback by the document?
2 What arguments does Cromwell offer in paragraphs II and III?
3 How effectively does Cromwell advance his arguments in paragraphs IV and V? Consider language, tone and content.
4 What evidence of Cromwell's opposition to the *Agreement* is contained in paragraph VI?

Explain, using your wider knowledge, Cromwell's comment in paragraph I that 'this paper does contain ... very great alterations'.

What Cromwell did

irm action within the army

.s the Debates progressed it became apparent that Leveller arguments vere winning the day. Cromwell decided to end the debate and 1stead hold an army rendezvous. This had been envisaged by the evellers as an occasion attended by all regiments where individuals ould sign up to the *Agreement*. Instead, the commanders held a series f separate rendezvous for groups of regiments and arranged for a 1uch less radical document to be presented. The unauthorised atten-ance of two regiments at the Ware rendezvous constituted the Ware 1utiny (page 43). Most authorities are agreed that Cromwell was per-onally active and effective in quelling this challenge.

◢ Source 2

romwell's bold and furious action [at Ware] was largely instrumental in cowing [the 1utineers] into submission and within a week the army's discipline and solidarity were ·iumphantly restored.

> A. Woolrych, 'Cromwell as Soldier' *in John Morrill (ed.),*
> ***Oliver Cromwell and the English revolution** (1990)*

◢ Source 3

·he Ware rendezvous was a notable victory for the Grandees. The seven regiments fficially summoned accepted the moderate policy statement without fuss; the two 1utinous regiments had wavered in the face of determined action; and discipline had een restored with a minimum of bloodshed. For the Levellers, it was a sharp setback. ▮lthough John Lilburne, recently released on bail, had hastened to Ware, Leveller ·lans had been uncoordinated ...

Indoubtedly the flight of the King had much to do with [their] indecision; the possibility ·f renewed civil war must have made any attack on the officers seem inopportune ... Jevertheless ... Corkbush Field (near Ware) was a major reverse. Having helped to ·ictate the pace and direction of events for the last six months, the Levellers found at ·his vital point that the New Model Army remained a disciplined body with a powerful ▮yalty to Fairfax and Cromwell.

> H. Shaw, ***The Levellers** (Longman, 1973)*

◢ Source 4

The soldiers allowed themselves to be overawed by the prestige of Fairfax and the sheer personality and courage of Cromwell. The 'mutiny' was suppressed at the cost of one soldier executed (out of three who were sentenced to die) and three officers arrested ... But the cost to the Leveller cause was in fact much heavier than this. For they had played their trump card – direct action by the rank-and-file of the army – and it had failed. As events turned out, they were to try it only once more, and then under even less favourable circumstance.

G. E. Aylmer, **The Levellers in the English Revolution** (Cornell University Press, 197?)

6 On the evidence of Sources 1–4, what significance would you attribute to Cromwell's response to the Levellers in October–November 1647?

How did the Levellers view Oliver Cromwell?

Cromwell faced many accusations from contemporaries of betrayal and hypocrisy in his dealing with friends and supporters. He was accused of making cynical use of them and then dropping them.

There were also accusations that he was unprincipled in his political dealings; that he believed that the end justified the means. In spite of the widespread criticism of unprincipled behaviour in his political life there was not a similar challenge to his religious sincerity. That in itself would appear to give more weight to the criticisms which were made since it does not appear that blanket attacks were made indiscriminately in the hope of discrediting him. However, these criticisms are made by frustrated and defeated men. How much weight should we place upon them?

It was in the autumn of 1647 that the Levellers began the attack on Cromwell's reputation. They campaigned in print vociferously until the movement effectively died out in 1649. But many of the accusations made then were repeated later. They were taken up by others as the events of 1653 (the dissolution of the Rump and the establishment of the Protectorate) aroused opposition.

Source 5

The proposals connive at ... the Lords' constant treasonable subversion of the fundamental laws of England by ... summoning ... and imprisoning the Commons, over whom by the known laws they have no original jurisdiction ...

And does not this practice run parallel with this proposal? Has not Cromwell suffered that Gallant champion for English freedom, Lieutenant-General John Lilburne, to consume in prison by that usurped lordly power? Yea, though Cromwell first engaged him against the lordly usurpation and tyranny, by impeaching the Earl of Manchester for his treachery; yet hath he not unworthily deserted both the prosecution of justice against him, and left his implored assistant alone to maintain the hazardous contest?

John Wildman, **Putney Projects** (1 August 1647)

Source 6

Was there ever a generation of men so Apostate, so false and so perjured as these? Did ever men pretend an higher degree of Holiness, Religion and Zeal to God and their Country than these? These preach, these fast, these pray, these have nothing more frequent than the sentences of sacred Scripture the Name of God and of Christ in their mouths: You will scarce speak to Cromwell about anything, but he will lay his hand on his breast, elevate his eyes and call God to record. He will weep, howl and repent even while he doth smite you under the first rib.

The Hunting of the Foxes published 21 March 1649, probably by Richard Overton. Here the accusation of hypocrisy is made even more openly

John Lilburne in particular felt betrayed by Cromwell. In *England's New Chains Discovered*, published in two parts in the spring of 1649, he attacked the new régime set up after the execution of the King. It is evident that the new executive authority is viewed with just as much suspicion as the old:

Source 7

For where is that good, or where is that liberty so much pretended, so deeply purchased? If we look upon what this House has done since it hath voted itself the Supreme Authority ...

First we find a high court of justice erected for the trial of criminal causes; whereby [trial by jury] ... is over-ruled by a Court consisting of persons picked in an unusual way ...

This is the first part of our new liberty ...

Then the stopping of our mouths from Printing is carefully provided for ... to gag us from discovering the truth and discovering the tyrannies of bad men ...

Those petitioners that have moved in behalf of the people ... [have had] ... empty thanks, their desires ... not at all considered; at other times meeting with ... violent motions, that their Petitions be burnt by the common hangman, whilst others are not taken in at all; to so small an account are the people brought, even while they are flattered with notions of being the Original of all just power.

And lastly, for compleating this new kind of liberty, a Council of State [is formed] possessed with power to ... imprison any that shall disobey their commands ... What now is become of that liberty that no man's person shall be ... imprisoned... but by lawful judgement of his equals ...

John Lilburne, ***England's New Chains Discovered*** *(164?*

After the publication of *England's New Chains Discovered* Lilburne wa arrested and brought before the Council of State. What survives i Lilburne's account of Cromwell's speech to the Council of State which was made after Lilburne was taken from the room, but which he over heard.

◢ Source 8

'I tell you sir,' Cromwell declared, thumping the table, 'you have no other way to deal with these men but to break them or they will break you; yea and bring all the guilt of the blood and treasure shed and spent in this kingdom upon your heads and shoulders and frustrate and make void all that work that, with so many years' industry, toil and pains you have done and so render you to all rational men in the world as the most contemptibilest generation of silly, low-spirited men in the earth to be broken and routed by such a despicable contemptible generation of men as they are, and therefore, sirs I tell you again you are necessitated to break them.'

Quoted in W. C. Abbott (ed.), ***The Writings and Speeches o****
Oliver Cromwell Volume 2 (1939*

1 Study Sources 5 and 6.
What contemporary events help explain these attacks on Cromwell?

Study Source 7 and refer to Chapters 3 and 5.

How far do the events and the constitutional and political changes of early 1649 warrant John Lilburne's description of 'New Chains Discovered'?

Study Source 8.

How credible do you feel Lilburne's account is? Consider Cromwell's earlier responses and reactions to the Levellers and his subsequent actions.

Judgements about Cromwell

◢ Source 9

He excused the execution done upon the soldier at the rendezvous [at Ware] as absolutely necessary to keep things from falling into confusion; which must have ensured upon that division, if it had not been timely prevented, he professed to desire nothing more than that the government of the nation might be settled in a free and equal commonwealth, acknowledging that there was no other probable means to keep the old family and government from returning upon us ...

This is from the memoirs of Edmund Ludlow, published in Switzerland in 1698. Ludlow was one of the signatories to the King's death warrant in 1649. He later accused Cromwell of abandoning the principles for which they had fought. Here he records a conversation in which Cromwell justified his response to the Levellers.

◢ Source 10

In the political crisis which followed the Second Civil War ... the Grandees contemptuously exploited and then cast aside the Levellers, 'of whom there is no fear' as Cromwell put it. Some of the forms recommended by the Levellers were adopted – a republic, abolition of the House of Lords – but none of the democratic content which alone, in the Leveller view, could have legitimated military intervention in politics. The Leveller leaders were arrested, the radical regiments provoked into unsuccessful mutiny, which was crushed at Burford in May 1649. Army democracy was finished. So, effectively were the Levellers.

Christopher Hill, ***The World Turned Upside Down*** (Penguin, 1972)

1 Study source 9. According to Ludlow, what explanation did Cromwell offer for his response to the Levellers in 1647?

2 Study source 10 and use the knowledge of Cromwell's actions and motives that you have gained from this Chapter to answer the following question:

In the context of the events of 1647–49, and the opportunities open to him, how far do Cromwell's responses to the Levellers suggest that he was essentially a social and political conservative?

CHAPTER FOUR

WAS CROMWELL A CONSTITUTIONAL RULER OR A MILITARY DICTATOR?

Objectives

◢ To understand Cromwell's motives in the search for a constitutional settlement, 1653–58

◢ To understand the reasons for his decisions and their outcomes

◢ To assess the nature of his position as Lord Protector.

Key events

1649	Rump Parliament sets up a Council of State (February)
	Act to abolish the monarchy (March)
	Act to abolish the House of Lords (March)
	Act declaring England to be a Commonwealth (May)
1649–50	Cromwell campaigns in Ireland
1650–51	Campaigns in Scotland
1653	Dissolves the Rump Parliament (20 April)
	Opens the Nominated Assembly (4 July)
	Installed as Lord Protector under the *Instrument of Government* (16 December)
1654	Opens first Protectorate Parliament (4 September)
1655	Appoints Major-Generals (August)
1656	Opens second Protectorate Parliament (September)
1657	Accepts *Humble Petition and Advice* but refuses offer of the crown (May)
	Second installation as Lord Protector (26 June)
1658	Dissolves second Protectorate Parliament (4 February)

1 The Dissolution of the Rump

The Rump Parliament

The execution of Charles I in January 1649 was followed by the abolition of both the monarchy and of the House of Lords. The purged House of Commons was now all that was left of the Long Parliament that had met in 1642. Its opponents were later to call it 'the Rump' and most historians still use that name. From 1649 to 1653 the Rump was both the government and the Parliament of a Commonwealth, or republic, which at first consisted of England and Wales and Ireland and later, from 1651, also included Scotland (see Chapter 6).

What were Cromwell's attitudes to the Rump?

1 Obedience

Cromwell looked upon the Rump as a body to be obeyed. In his eyes it was the supreme power in the land. Its members had sat continuously since 1642. They may have been only a remnant of the original membership of the Long Parliament, but they still formed a legitimate Parliament and held the right to exercise authority. To that authority the army should defer.

2 Settlement

Cromwell did not see the Rump as a permanent institution. Its tasks were:

- to establish the new Commonwealth;
- to organise a successor Parliament that would be more representative.

In 1651, under pressure from Cromwell, the Rump voted to dissolve itself not later than November 1654. A month later, at a conference about a future constitution, Cromwell was reported to say that 'a settlement of somewhat of a monarchical power in it would be very effectual' and to be interested in the idea that one of Charles I's sons, possibly the Duke of Gloucester, might be admitted to the throne.

The problem was that many in the army were impatient to get rid of the Rump. They were dissatisfied with its attitude to religious and social reform and therefore wanted to force it to dissolve at once. Cromwell's great concern was that any future Parliament or constitution should be set up by Parliament, the legitimate civil power, not by the army. Throughout 1652 and early 1653 he successfully manoeuvred to protect the Rump from the more radical members of the Council of Officers.

3 Support

It is a strong indication of Cromwell's conservative instincts in constitutional matters that as well as considering a settlement with 'somewhat of a monarchical power' in it, he disagreed with the abolition of the House of Lords. He believed this would alienate many important figures in the land whose support was essential to the new régime. In the 1640s he had worked closely with Independent peers in the Lords and was respectful of their authority and influence. It had been a blow to him that they had refused to support the trial and execution of the King. It was men like these who he particularly wanted to win round to active support of the Commonwealth.

His aim was to build up the broadest possible base of support for the new Commonwealth. As well as wanting to win over his old Independent allies he hoped to reconcile Presbyterians and Independents in Parliament. He spoke in favour of allowing MPs still excluded from the House after the Pride's Purge to be re-admitted, and he successfully campaigned to alter the oath of allegiance so that those taking it did not have to express approval of the purge and execution.

4 Reform

At the same time Cromwell looked to the Rump to bring about the reforms in religion and society which he associated with the Parliamentary cause. Between 1649 and 1651 victories against the Irish and Scots (see Chapter 6) convinced him that God approved of the execution of the King and was on the side of the newly created Commonwealth. Once again the combination of living among soldiers of radical religious and social views and the experience of military victory reinforced Cromwell's beliefs and his passion for change. Writing to the Speaker after his remarkable victory over the Scots at Dunbar he urged Parliament to 'relieve the oppressed, hear the groans of the poor prisoners in England; be pleased to reform the abuses of all professions; and if there be any one that makes many poor to make a few rich, that suits not a Commonwealth.'

After defeating the Royalist army at Worcester Cromwell wrote that the victory was 'for aught I know a crowning mercy' and urged Parliament: 'to do the will of Him [i.e. God] who hath done His will for it, and for the Nation; – whose good pleasure it is to establish the Nation and the Change of Government.'

Cromwell and the godly now looked to the Rump to institute far-reaching reforms. Their demands included:

◢ religion – freedom of worship for orthodox sects such as the

Independents and a nationwide programme to appoint godly ministers, promote preaching and spread the gospel;

◢ the law – fundamental changes in its administration to make the use of the courts cheaper and easier for both ordinary people and regular users such as landowners and merchants;

◢ social improvements – action to spread education and help the poor.

Why did Cromwell dissolve the Rump?

In March 1653 relations between the army and the Rump reached a low point. Various radical officers again proposed to dismiss the Rump by force, but Cromwell managed to prevent them. He argued that if the army called a new Parliament then 'the Parliament is not the supreme power, but that is the supreme power that calls it'. Shortly afterwards he was absent from Parliament for several weeks. Then, on 19 April, he called another conference between officers and MPs who appeared to reach a compromise about the arrangements for calling a new Parliament. Yet the very next day Cromwell himself stood up in the House and roundly condemned the members of the Rump before calling in troops and telling the MPs to leave for good: 'You have sat here too long for the good you do. In the name of God, go!' Why did Cromwell suddenly do the very thing he had spent so much time and energy trying to prevent?

1 Failure to reform

There is no doubt that although Cromwell stood between the army and Parliament until the last minute, he shared the frustration of many of his officers that the Rump was slow to implement the reforms they expected of it. In fact the Rump did carry out some reforms. For example, it reduced the punishment given to poor debtors, allowed English rather than Latin or French to be used in law courts, repealed an Elizabethan law making weekly churchgoing compulsory and passed Acts to spread the gospel in Wales and Ireland. A Blasphemy Act attempted to restore the religious discipline which many feared was breaking down with the proliferation of religious sects such as Ranters (page 87), **Seekers** and Baptists (page 85). An Adultery Act likewise aimed to impose moral discipline by giving JPs powers previously exercised by the Church courts which had fallen into disuse following the abolition of bishops.

KEY TERM

Seekers believed that God made Himself known as a divine spirit working within each individual. Therefore they set out to 'seek' Him by responding to their own inner promptings. They also believed that no true Church existed and that everyone should wait until God chose to establish one.

None of these actions, however, went far enough or fast enough for godly reformers. Many even suspected that in the case of law reform some MPs were out to prevent major changes. So Cromwell was certainly disappointed with the Rump's record; but it is unlikely that this alone would have caused him to take such drastic action on 20 April.

2 A broken agreement

It was the events of 19–20 April which triggered Cromwell's action. At the meeting between officers and MPs on 19 April it was agreed that the next day the Rump would dissolve itself and hand over power to a council chosen by the army. This council would then make arrangements for a new Parliament. Because it was to be dominated by officers it would be able to ensure that the new Parliament would be full of godly MPs, favourable to the army's ideas for reform.

But the next day the Rump voted for something completely different and it was this breaking of the agreement of the day before that provoked Cromwell into calling in his troops and dismissing the MPs. Historians used to think that the Rump had decided never to dissolve. It is difficult to be sure because Cromwell took away the only copy of the Bill that they were debating. Now, however, as a result of detective work by Blair Worden, historians think that the very opposite was true: the Rump had at last voted to dissolve itself and call new elections. In theory this was what Cromwell had wanted all along: in practice he knew that elections held outside the army's control would return MPs hostile to reform. The whole point of the agreement reached the day before had been to make sure that the next Parliament would be in tune with the army. Faced with this vote Cromwell turned on the Rump.

3 A new legitimacy

Since 1648 Cromwell's attitude towards Parliament had been slowly changing. As he became more convinced that the army was God's chosen instrument in moulding the affairs of the nation, he had difficulty in continuing to see Parliament as a supreme power that had to be obeyed unconditionally. Instead he formed the view that Parliament should be obeyed as long as it held true to the trust placed in it to rule according to God's will. When he explained the expulsion of the Rump to the Nominated Assembly, or 'Barebone's Parliament', he told its members that he had come to believe that the army and not the Rump stood for the godly cause. That was why, in the end, the army had the right to dismiss the Rump and replace it with an assembly that might govern in a godly manner.

The consequences

1 The role of Parliament

Cromwell had broken with his long-held view of Parliament's rights and authority. Although he remained committed to the importance of Parliament as a civil authority, he no longer saw it as the supreme power in the land. He had replaced a constitutional idea of Parliament with a religious one which said that Parliament had to rule according to God's will as interpreted by the godly.

2 The role of the army

Since Cromwell believed that the army represented the godly, it followed that he had now committed himself to a constitution that would be created, and monitored, by the army. Although the army had been in effective control since 1648, Cromwell's hope had been that it would be Parliament which established the next government. After the expulsion of the Rump it was obvious to all that in practice it was the army which held supreme power.

3 Cromwell and the radicals

The expulsion of the Rump restored Cromwell's popularity with the army and with Independent congregations in the country. Both groups had been frustrated by his endless attempts to negotiate a deal with MPs, and the views of officers hostile to the Rump had been rapidly gaining ground in the army. Without doubt Cromwell's actions on 20 April put him back in favour with his brother officers and their troops. Once again he was in full control of the army.

4 The Nominated Assembly

The fact that Cromwell had no plans in place for a successor body to the Rump suggests that his decision to dismiss it was made in some haste. After ten days the Council of Officers announced that the authority to carry out day-to-day government would temporarily pass to a new ten-man Council of State (seven of whom were army officers) while arrangements were made to set up a new supreme power. This was to be an assembly of about 140 people 'fearing God and of approved integrity and honesty'. They were not to be elected but to be nominated by Cromwell and the Council of Officers. There would be representatives from Ireland and Scotland as well as from England and Wales. In July 1653 the Nominated Assembly met for the first time and, against Cromwell's wishes, promptly declared itself to be a Parliament.

Cromwell's aims and attitudes

1 A compromise

Historians used to think that the calling of the Nominated Assembly showed that Cromwell had been won over to the views of the millenarian Major-General John Harrison, leader of the *Fifth Monarchists*. Harrison wanted an assembly set up on the lines of the Saahedria, the council of the ancient Israelites. About 70 godly men would be chosen by the Independent Churches to rule the country until the expected return to earth of Jesus Christ.

In fact Cromwell appears to have compromised between this view and that of General John Lambert (page 19) who wanted the Council of Officers to choose a small council to run the country while a new constitution was drawn up. Harrison's ideas were rejected in several crucial respects. The Assembly was far larger than he wanted. It was appointed by the army not by Independent congregations, and a time-limit was set on its existence. It was to complete its work and dissolve in November 1654.

KEY TERM

Fifth Monarchists were a group in the 1650s who believed that the Fifth Monarchy predicted in the Bible was about to happen. During the Fifth Monarchy Christ would join his Saints to rule on earth for a thousand years. Fifth Monarchists thought it was their duty to prepare for this with radical reforms.

2 His vision

Cromwell did, however, expect the 'Saints' chosen to sit in the Nominated Assembly to carry out the 'godly reformation' for which he craved. He believed that they would succeed where the Rump had failed and implement a programme of religious and social reforms. When he addressed the Assembly at its opening he was in a state of passionate optimism: 'I confess I never looked to see such a day as this – it may be nor you neither – when Jesus Christ should be so owned as He is, at this day, and in this work ... I say, you are called with a high call.'

3 His personal position

If Cromwell had actually intended to set up a military dictatorship there was no better time to do it than after his dismissal of the Rump. The fact that he immediately handed power over to another body suggests that he genuinely wished to achieve non-military government. He later claimed the episode was 'a story of my own folly and weakness'; but, at the time, the fact that he refused a seat either in the Assembly or on the Council of State indicated the strength both of his belief that the Nominated Assembly was the right solution, and of his faith in its members.

4 Elected Parliaments

Cromwell continued to believe in the importance of elected Parliaments. He did not see the Nominated Assembly as a long-term constitutional solution. One of its tasks was to find a constitutional settlement based on an elected Parliament. Cromwell's hope was that once the Nominated Assembly had given people a taste of the benefits of godly rule electors would want to vote for godly MPs in the future.

Why did the Assembly dissolve?

The Assembly's enemies soon nicknamed it the 'Barebone's Parliament' after a supposedly typical member, a London leather-seller called Praise-God Barebones. Historians used to believe, as contemporary critics claimed, that it consisted of inexperienced men from humble backgrounds full of crazy and impractical notions of reform. Recent research suggests otherwise. It is true that compared to a normal Parliament a greater proportion of members were minor gentry. Also about 12 members were Fifth Monarchists. But overall the picture is of a group of people from propertied backgrounds and with plenty of administrative experience. About two-thirds of them were gentry; the same proportion were JPs; and well over half had been to university or had trained as lawyers.

Historians also now believe that the Assembly managed to do a good deal of useful work. It attempted to improve the tax system and financial administration. It passed laws to allow the civil registration of births, marriages and deaths which previously had had to be done by Church courts. It legislated for a more humane treatment for people judged to be insane. It reformed the laws on debt. It discussed the unification of Ireland, Scotland and England and law reform.

Why then did a group of representatives go to Cromwell in December 1653, 11 months before the Nominated Assembly was due to dissolve, and hand back the authority he had given them?

1 Fear of the extremists

Like Cromwell himself, most members of the Assembly held opinions on issues such as religion and social reform which the majority of gentlemen in the country as a whole regarded as radical. A few members, however, mainly from sects such as the Fifth Monarchists, held views which even their colleagues in the Assembly found extreme. This small but vociferous minority soon gave the Assembly a bad name by making proposals which offended moderates and conservatives alike by attacking the rights of property owners and the traditional ways of keeping social discipline. Two of the chief culprits were proposals to:

- produce a code book of laws and, in the process, abandon much of England's traditional common law;
- abolish the tithe system which at the time was the only way of paying Church ministers. In addition, by this time many tithes were going not to the upkeep of ministers but into the pockets of landlords as rent. So these landlords were strongly opposed to any change.

2 Cromwell's role

Cromwell later claimed he had no idea that members of the Assembly were going to hand back their power to him in December. This seems improbable; but even if true it is highly likely that the moderates in the

Assembly were well aware that Cromwell had become thoroughly disillusioned with it. It was bad enough that the extremists were busily alienating the support of the country gentlemen whom Cromwell had hoped would be won over to the new government. It was worse when they came up with a plan to abolish the monthly assessment, the tax which paid for the standing army. If the tax went, so did the army and with it the Saints-in-arms on whom, if all else failed, Cromwell's hopes for godly rule were pinned.

3 The reaction of the moderates

The end came as a result of a neat plot involving about 40 moderates. Taking advantage of the absence of the extremists at a prayer meeting, they voted to leave the chamber and resign their authority to Cromwell. Almost certainly they knew that Cromwell would approve.

4 The Protectorate

This time the Council of Officers was prepared. John Lambert had been working on a new written constitution. After making some amendments Cromwell accepted the Instrument of Government and the title of Lord Protector (Figure 3). Once again a constitutional settlement had been imposed by the army; once again the hope among Cromwell and his officers was that it would allow the army to fade in to the background.

Cromwell's aims and attitudes

1 'Healing and settling'

At this time Cromwell frequently spoke of 'healing and settling'. One of his main aims was to try to please the great majority of property owners who had yet to reconcile themselves to the destruction of the monarchy. Such people needed reassurance that his régime would protect the rights of property and ensure social discipline. Speaking to his first Parliament Cromwell made a point of criticising 'Levelling principles' and underlined his traditional view of the hierarchy of society when he told MPs, 'a nobleman, a gentleman, and a yeoman, that is a good interest of the nation and a great one'. Meanwhile the dismissal of Major-General Harrison confirmed the move away from the ideas associated with the extremists in the Nominated Assembly. Also, more civilians than officers were appointed to the new Council of State. Meanwhile Cromwell was lenient towards many Royalists, some of whom were allowed to buy back their confiscated estates.

LORD PROTECTOR

Cromwell was appointed
Lord Protector for life

Powers:
- rule with the advice, and on major issues the consent, of the Council of State
- share control of the militia with the Council and with Parliament (when sitting)
- share control of the standing army with the Council
- with the Council's approval use the money from customs and other sources for 'ordinary' expenditure
- veto any proposal that was likely to overturn the fundamental principles of the Instrument

STANDING ARMY

A standing army of 30,000 soldiers to be jointly controlled by the Protector and Parliament

COUNCIL OF STATE

Up to 21 members

Powers:
- appoint Cromwell's successor as Protector
- advise the Protector on all aspects of policy and administration
- its consent needed on major issues
- appoint its own members
- share control of militia with the Protector and Parliament (when sitting)
- share control of standing army with the Protector

NATIONAL CHURCH

- To teach 'sound doctrine'
- Liberty of worship to be granted to 'such as profess faith in God by Jesus Christ'; but not to Roman Catholics or those guilty of 'licentiousness'

PARLIAMENT

- A single chamber only
- 400 MPs for England and Wales; 30 for Scotland; 30 for Ireland
- MPs to be 'of known integrity, fearing God and of good conversation'
- Had to be in session for five months every three years

Powers:
- recommend names for new councillors to the Council
- share control of militia with the Protector and Council
- no taxes to be raised without its consent

Elected by
Men with property or income valued at £200 or over. This excluded modest property owners previously entitled to vote (the 40-shilling freeholders). Roman Catholics and known Royalists were debarred from voting or standing for election

Figure 3 Key features of the Instrument of Government

2 The role of Protector

The new constitution with its Single Person and Parliament reflected the ideas of the *Heads of the Proposals* and sought to put checks on the power of both sides (Figure 3). It also demanded considerable cooperation between the Protector and the Council of State. Although evidence of this is scarce, recent research suggests that, while Cromwell was clearly the dominant figure and capable of acting independently, he also frequently listened to his Councillors' advice.

Originally Lambert had wanted Cromwell to become King; but Cromwell refused to go down that path believing that God had signalled his disapproval of kingship. He did, however, combine some of the trappings of monarchy with his own down-to-earth style. He lived in the old Royal palaces which had their works of art restored to them. He received foreign ambassadors ceremonially as well as informally. He was called 'Your Highness' and where Charles I had signed himself 'Charles R' (Charles Rex) Cromwell adopted the signature 'Oliver P' (Oliver Protector).

3 Reform

Although anxious to increase support for his régime, Cromwell did not abandon his plan to achieve godly reform. In particular he was keen to reform the law and to ensure both freedom of conscience and a godly ministry (see Chapter 5).

The first Protectorate Parliament

The Instrument of Government allowed the Protector and the Council to rule as they saw fit until the first Parliament. It was the first Parliament's job to agree the Instrument and so put the government on a proper constitutional footing.

1 Disputes

The elections returned a majority of MPs who for different reasons disapproved of what Cromwell and the army had done since 1647. Many were Political Presbyterians who believed a settlement should have been reached with Charles I. Some were republicans angry about the dissolution of the Rump. Most had a quarrel with some aspect of the Instrument: so instead of ratifying it they proceeded to criticise it. There were complaints that Parliament's position was too weak and the Protector's too strong; that the standing army was too large and therefore too expensive; and that the Instrument allowed too great a degree of religious toleration.

2 Purge

Angry that Parliament was thwarting his two-part agenda of 'healing and settling' and reform, Cromwell intervened to demand that MPs should swear their allegiance to the Protectorate. In the process he outlined the four 'fundamentals' on which he believed the constitution should rest:

- government should be by a Single Person and Parliament;
- Parliaments should not be permanent but should meet frequently;
- there should be freedom of conscience in religion;
- control of the militia should be shared between the Single Person and Parliament.

A hundred MPs withdrew rather than take the oath. Another Parliament had, therefore, been purged; but such was the strength of feeling among MPs that it made little difference. The criticisms continued. MPs first attempted to limit freedom of conscience by banning the beliefs of various sects which were thought to threaten social discipline, then they blocked the monthly assessment which paid for the army. Anxious to get rid of Parliament as quickly as possible, Cromwell effectively cheated by dissolving it after five lunar months instead of five of the longer calendar months which the constitution clearly intended.

The consequences

1 The role of the army

Cromwell had dissolved Parliament partly because of its attack on the army. In his dissolution speech he made clear just how vital the army still was to his position:

◢ Source

It determines his [the Protector's] power, either for doing the good he aught, or hindering Parliaments from perpetuating themselves, or from imposing what religions they please on the consciences of men, or what government they please on the nation.

*W. C. Abbott (ed.), **The Writings and Speeches of Oliver Cromwell**, Volume 3 (1937–47)*

2 Cromwell's isolation

The problem was that the majority in the country did not share Cromwell's vision of the army's role. Ordinary people were tired of soldiers and resented having them stationed in their localities. Propertied people resented paying for their upkeep. Only a minority had supported the army's actions since 1647 and, since then, Cromwell himself had progressively turned his own allies into enemies. He had lost the support first of the Political Independents over the purge and regicide (1648–49); then of the Levellers (1649); then of republicans angered by the dissolution of the Rump (1653); and most recently of the Fifth Monarchists and other millenarian radicals angered by the dissolution of the Nominated Assembly.

3 An unratified constitution

Parliament had not ratified the new constitution. According to the Instrument's own clauses, therefore, Cromwell's government had no authority to continue. It did continue, of course, and it was generally obeyed; but it remained a government installed by the army alone.

4 Authoritarian rule

Frustrated by Parliament Cromwell abandoned ideas of settlement and embarked upon a phase of increasingly authoritarian rule. He was motivated partly by fears of Royalist plots and partly by the religious conviction that he was simply acting for the good of the people. As a result he began to react to opposition much as Charles I had done in the 1630s. When the government was challenged in the law courts he dismissed judges who found against it. He argued that for reasons of state he was entitled to imprison people without trial. Whatever Cromwell's motives, these actions were arbitrary and illegal. Cromwell described them as 'necessities', but as Ronald Hutton has pointed out 'the inventions mothered by necessity are commonly crimes'.

The Major-Generals, 1655–57

In early 1655 Cromwell commissioned Major-General John Desborough, his brother-in-law, to deal with a Royalist uprising in the west country led by Penruddock. The rebellion turned out to be poorly organised and weakly supported. It was easily crushed. Nevertheless it gave impetus to Cromwell's next experiment which was to add a new layer to local government. By summer 1655 he had divided England and Wales into 11 regions (later 12) and put a Major-General in charge of running each one.

Cromwell's aims and attitudes

1 Security

Despite the weakness of Penruddock's Rising Cromwell remained concerned about the threat of Royalist uprisings. One of the Major-Generals' chief tasks was to look after local security. They were also to raise militia locally in the hope that the size, and therefore cost, of the standing army could be reduced.

2 Reform

The Major-Generals were also charged with reform of public morals (see Chapter 5). Cromwell's hope was that a godly society could be achieved through the direct efforts of godly rulers in the localities. Partly this was an attempt to achieve a longstanding goal; but it was given additional drive by Cromwell's recently formed belief that God was displeased with the nation because its people were sinful and unreformed. He had come to this conclusion as a result of the failure of the Western Design, a plan to attack Spanish possessions in the Caribbean. Cromwell interpreted its failure as a providence which showed God's disfavour towards a nation which until now He had blessed with success. It became a matter of urgency to regain God's favour with a programme that reformed people's morals and behaviour.

3 Royalists

To pay for their work the Major-Generals were to raise a Decimation Tax, a ten per cent charge on Royalists with incomes of £100 a year or more. The use of this levy suggests a reversal of Cromwell's earlier policy of compromise towards Royalists.

Results

1 The appointment of the Major-Generals emphasised the military nature of Cromwell's régime.

2 Their rule was very unpopular:

◢ local gentry resented the interference in local government of men who were (a) soldiers and (b) generally of lower social status than themselves;

◢ people of all sorts resented 'godly' attempts to end traditional pastimes, customs and entertainments (see Chapter 5);

◢ Royalists who had not been not actively hostile towards Cromwell were alienated by the Decimation Tax.

3 Although Cromwell claimed that the Major-Generals' reforming efforts were a great success, historians tend to disagree (see Chapter 5). In any case, with the calling of his second Parliament Cromwell returned to a policy of 'healing and settling'. In 1657, following opposition to the renewal of the Decimation Tax, he quietly allowed the rule of the Major-Generals to lapse.

The offer of the crown

The background

1 A new mood

During 1656–57 a new group of advisers appears to have risen to prominence around Cromwell. They were civilians rather than soldiers and chief among them was Lord Broghill, a former Royalist who had served Cromwell in both Ireland and Scotland (see page 19) and was now one of his closest confidants. Broghill and his group put political stability ahead of ideology. They believed that most Royalists and Political Presbyterians would accept the new régime if only Cromwell would tone down his reforming zeal and end his reliance on the army. Their plan was to persuade Cromwell to become King thereby elevating him as a national leader and at the same time putting an end to military rule and placing traditional controls upon his power. Their greatest fear was that Cromwell might die and his place as Lord Protector be taken by his natural successor, the dynamic General Lambert, who would perpetuate the military régime.

2 Nayler's case

Broghill's group had many supporters in the second Protectorate Parliament which Cromwell called in late 1656 largely because he needed extra money to fight a war against Spain. Once again he had intervened to prevent over a hundred elected members from taking their seats on the grounds that they were unsuitable, but this did not prevent a potentially serious clash between Protector and Parliament.

It arose over the case of James Nayler, a Quaker (see page 86), who rode into Bristol on a donkey in a re-enactment of Christ's entry into Jerusalem on the first Palm Sunday.

Appalled MPs pronounced Nayler's behaviour to be a 'horrid blasphemy' and condemned him to a series of harsh punishments. Cromwell almost certainly shared the MPs' view of Nayler's actions but was even more concerned about the implications of theirs:

◢ many MPs made no distinction between Nayler's opinions and those of other sects, including the Independents, whose rights Cromwell wished to protect;

◢ in dealing with the case MPs had found ways round the fact that it was the Protector's job under the Instrument to preserve liberty of conscience. Nayler's case convinced Cromwell that in order to preserve liberty of conscience in the face of intolerant Parliaments, changes had to be made to the constitution. The solution he favoured was a second Parliamentary chamber, along the lines of the old House of Lords, with powers to check the first chamber.

The Humble Petition and Advice

In March 1657 Parliament presented Cromwell with proposals for a new constitution. Under the Humble Petition and Advice:

◢ Cromwell would become hereditary King with sufficient money to govern;

◢ a powerful Council of State would advise him;

◢ regular Parliaments would have to approve appointments to the great offices of state and all taxation, and would share control of the armed forces with the monarch;

◢ a second chamber of Parliament would be nominated by the King and the Council;

◢ religious freedom would be denied to those who promoted 'horrid blasphemies' or 'licentiousness and profaness'.

Cromwell's decision

Cromwell was tempted by the Humble Petition. It dealt with several of the Instrument's weaknesses. It was put forward by Parliament and would, therefore, clearly be legal. Acceptance of the crown would almost certainly have won his régime the broad range of support among the gentry that he had been anxious to achieve for so long. Yet after weeks of indecision he told Parliament that, 'although I think the government doth consist of very excellent parts, in all but that one thing, the title ... I am persuaded to return this answer to you, that I cannot undertake this government with the title of King'. What drove him to that unexpected conclusion?

1 The army
The army was implacably opposed to the Humble Petition and Advice and Lambert led a campaign to persuade Cromwell to reject it. The soldiers particularly objected to the idea of another King when, they claimed, they had fought the Civil War to get rid of the last one. It used to be argued that Cromwell rejected the crown largely because of the political reality that the army would not go along with him; but, more recently, historians have disputed this. They point out that even senior figures such as Lambert did nothing more serious than threaten to resign if Cromwell accepted the crown, and that Cromwell's control of the army was as secure as ever at this time. Had he wanted to, he could have overcome, or overridden, the soldiers' objections.

2 Godly reformation
It seems more likely that what influenced Cromwell most was the strong feeling among godly people, both in the army itself and within the sects, that to accept the crown would amount to a betrayal of the cause of godly reformation. The fact was that by becoming King Cromwell would be forced to identify with, and respond to, the majority in the country who had no interest whatsoever in living godly lives and having their lives reformed as the Saints saw best for them. That, of course, was exactly what Broghill and his colleagues intended. Cromwell's dilemma was stark. If he accepted the crown he would gain the political consensus for which he hungered; but he would have to live with the fact that he no longer had the power to promote the cause of the Saints. Faced with the choice, he opted, as always in the past, for the cause of the Saints.

3 God's will
Nevertheless the decision was hard. As ever Cromwell searched his heart to try to discover God's will, and the evidence suggests that the failure of the Western Design continued to have a powerful affect upon

him. Cromwell feared that it was a providence which indicated God's displeasure in him as a person and as a leader. He became convinced that to accept the crown would be an act of personal self-aggrandisment which would find favour neither with the Saints nor with God. For God had already provided ample indication that it was His will that the office of King should be abolished: 'It hath been an issue of some ten or twelve years civil war wherin much blood hath been shed ... I will not seek to set up that that providence hath destroyed and laid in the dust ....'

The consequences

1 A revised constitution

Cromwell was soon offered an amended version of the Humble Petition and Advice under which he remained Lord Protector. He was installed for the second time in a splendid ceremony with strongly monarchical overtones. Despite Cromwell's refusal of the crown, for many the new constitution remained a retrograde step. Lambert was dismissed for refusing to take an oath of allegiance. An upsurge of criticism in the House of Commons from republicans hostile to the new 'Other House', as the second chamber was to be known, caused Cromwell to dismiss Parliament after a few weeks. Similar dissatisfactions in the army led him to dismiss six officers.

2 Squaring the circle

If the new constitution offended men like Lambert, there was some hope that it might appeal to the majority of the nation. The truth was, however, that although it was a civil constitution established by Parliament, a standing army remained in place and officers retained an influence on affairs. Cromwell had not felt able to concede to the desires of the majority who wanted an end to armies and to the threat of godly rule. The Saints-in-arms remained available as guardians of the godly cause. Cromwell genuinely wanted two things: a constitutional settlement; and godly reform. He could not have both: they were incompatible. In 1658 he died, as he had lived for the past five years, trying to square the circle.

Interpretation and evaluation of source material

When you are asked to interpret and evaluate a source you have to consider what conclusions can be drawn from it and what use the historian can make of it.

To interpret and evaluate a source well you need to consider three aspects:

◢ what you know or are told about the source;

◢ what you can work out from its content;

◢ what light your own knowledge of the historical context sheds on it.

There are a number of key questions which you can ask of sources to help you to analyse them and to consider them critically. This exercise is to help you do that. First read this source and then apply to it the questions that follow.

◢ Source

Cromwell and his army grew wanton with their power, and invented a thousand tricks of government, which, when nobody opposed, they themselves fell to dislike and vary every day. First he calls a Parliament out of his own pocket, himself naming a sort of godly man for every county, who meeting and not agreeing, a part of them, in the name of the people, gave up sovereignty to him. Shortly after he makes up several sorts of mock Parliaments, but not finding one of them absolutely to his turn, turned them off again. He soon quitted himself of his triumvirs, and first thrust out Harrison, then took away Lambert's commission, and would have been King but for fear of quitting his generalship. He weeded, in a few months' time, above a hundred and fifty godly officers out of the army, with whom many of the religious soldiers went off, and in their room abundance of the King's dissolute soldiers were entertained; and the army was almost changed from that godly religious army, whose valour God had crowned with triumph, into the dissolute army they had beaten, bearing yet a better name. His wife and children were setting up for principality, which suited no better with any of them than scarlet on the ape; only, to speak the truth of himself, he had much natural greatness, and well became the place he had usurped.

> From ***The Memoirs of the Life of Colonel John Hutchinson***. *These memoirs were written by his wife Lucy in 1664–67 but were not published until 1806. Until then they remained in her family's private library. Colonel Hutchinson was one of the regicides*

1 Using the information about the source

   a *Origin*. Who was Lucy Hutchinson and what bearing might this have on her views of Cromwell?

   b *Context of the writing*. How might the time of writing (i.e. after the Restoration) affect what is written, and does it appear to have done so?

   c *Audience and purpose*. What is implied by the title and nature of the source? What bearing does this have on the way in which we view its contents?

2 Using the internal evidence of the source

   a *Language and tone*. Have these been used throughout the source to create an impression? For example: What impression is conveyed by 'wanton' and 'tricks' in the first sentence?

   b *Selection and treatment of content*. What information has Lucy Hutchinson chosen to include? Which of Cromwell's actions have been selected and in what ways have they been represented? What image is conveyed, for example, by the use of 'mock Parliaments'. What is revealed about Lucy Hutchinson's own standpoint?

   c *Validity*. Does the author offer any evidence in support of the views and comments?

3 Interpreting the source in the context of your own knowledge and/or other evidence

   a *Meaning*. What is the author referring to? Can you explain each reference, e.g. '... he calls a Parliament out of his own pocket ...'?

   b *Accuracy*. How far is the information in the source supported by other evidence? Compare Lucy Hutchinson's account of events with that given in this chapter.

4 Evaluation of the source

   a *Reliability*. Taking into account the origin, purpose and content of the source, how much reliance can be placed on it? For example, what weight would you give to Lucy Hutchinson's view that '... he had much natural greatness, and well became the place he had usurped'?

   b *Utility*. Taking into account its origin, purpose and content, what use can the historian make of the source?

5 Class debate and essay

Was Cromwell a constitutional ruler or a military dictator?

Divide into two teams, one to argue that Cromwell was a constitutional ruler, the other to argue that he was a military dictator. Remember that in a debate you need to think through your opponents' case as well as your own so that you can counter their arguments. Start preparing your case by reading this chapter and making notes for and against your own side of the argument. Use a chart like this:

Cromwell was a military dictator	
Arguments for	**Arguments against**
Dissolution of the Rump: a military coup led by Cromwell.	He was driven to this by frustration over reform, and did it reluctantly.

Obviously the chart will read differently if you are arguing that Cromwell was a constitutional ruler.

You should concentrate most of your arguments on Cromwell as Lord Protector; but you will also need to consider what his earlier actions involving the Rump and the Nominated Assembly reveal about his attitudes and motives.

Once you have held the debate, write your own essay on the topic.

CHAPTER FIVE

OW FAR DID CROMWELL SUCCEED IN ESTABLISHING A GODLY NATION?

Objectives

◢ To understand Cromwell's attitudes and aims in the following areas:
1 'liberty of conscience'
2 a National Church
3 the reform of behaviour
4 social reform

◢ To examine and assess his achievements

◢ To examine the arts under the Protectorate and Cromwell's attitude to them.

Key events

1653	Cromwell accepts the *Instrument of Government* (December)
1654	Issues ordinance to set up the Triers (March)
	Issues ordinance to set up the Ejectors (August)
	Issues ordinance to reform the Court of Chancery
1655	Appoints the Major-Generals
1656	Nayler's case
	Performance of the opera 'The Siege of Rhodes' by Sir William Davenant
1657	Cromwell accepts the revised *Humble Petition and Advice*

Liberty of conscience

1 Cromwell and religious toleration

Liberty of conscience' was central to all the army's proposals for a peace settlement after the Civil War, and in 1654 Cromwell declared it to be one of his four 'fundamentals': those aspects of the constitution which he was on no account prepared to see altered. Historians used to assume that by 'liberty of conscience' he meant much the same as 'religious toleration'. Looking at his record as Protector, they saw that he allowed far more people to worship freely than either before the Interregnum or for a long time after it. They praised him for holding views ahead of his time.

Recently, however, historians have followed Blair Worden in arguing that religious toleration is a modern, liberal idea not applicable to Cromwell's thought at all. It is an attitude of mind which holds that the state should allow people to worship (or not) as they please either because different religious beliefs may be equally valid, or because people's beliefs are their own affair and not of public concern. Cromwell held neither of these views.

2 Cromwell's beliefs

Cromwell's passionate conviction that, with certain exceptions, people should be allowed to worship God in their own way, was based not on tolerance but on firmly held beliefs about 'godliness' and its central significance for the life of every person in the land. Cromwell believed that:

1 It was of supreme importance to each individual that he or she should find their own relationship with God and thus become 'saved'. Their inner belief was what was important. The exact outward form of their worship was immaterial.

2 Different people might find their way to God by different routes. Along the way a person might become involved in a wrong belief, but they should not be condemned for that if they were genuinely seeking God. As he told the Nominated Assembly, '. . . if the poorest Christian, the most mistaken Christian, shall desire to live peaceably and quietly under you – I say, if any shall desire to lead a life of godliness and honesty, let him be protected.'

3 God would help those who were seeking Him. It was not up to humans to intervene in this process by banning certain beliefs unless those beliefs were either socially disruptive or constituted a heresy.

4 Above all, God wanted all true believers to live together in unity, not to divide into rival Churches and sects. Freedom of worship would help to bring this about. As he wrote to Robert Hammond in 1648, 'I profess to thee I desire it in my heart, I have prayed for it, I have waited for the day to see union and right understanding between the godly people (Scots, English, Jews, Gentiles, Presbyterians, Independents, Anabaptists, and all)'. Thus Cromwell believed in the principle of 'liberty of conscience' not because he supported the idea of religious diversity, but because it would lead to the saving of souls and to unity among Protestants.

3 The defence of liberty
Against Presbyterians

Cromwell's chief problem in promoting liberty of conscience was that those who should have been its chief advocates and beneficiaries turned out to be its worst enemies. He expected to find the 'people of God' chiefly among Presbyterians and Independents (page 37) and **Baptists**, for he believed that despite outward differences the members of these groups shared the beliefs essential to salvation. Yet he found that Presbyterian MPs appeared mainly interested in hounding those of other persuasions, especially Baptists. In 1655 he castigated them for their urge to 'put their finger upon their brethren's consciences, to pinch them there'. 'What greater hypocrisy', he asked, 'than for those who were oppressed by the Bishops to become the greatest oppressors themselves, so soon as their yoke was removed?' He was continually frustrated that his vision of unity was not shared by the very people called to realise it: 'Where shall we find men of a universal spirit? Everyone desires to have liberty, but none will give it.'

KEY TERM

Baptists believed that religious faith was the result of personal experience. It could not be taught or learnt. Therefore, infant baptism was pointless. By contrast, adult baptism was the mark of a person's acceptance of Christ and was essential if a person was to become a Church member. Baptists saw no need for an organised church with priests or ministers. They were attacked by religious and political conservatives who unfairly associated them with the Anabaptists, a sixteenth-century German sect which had been involved in political and social protest.

Against the sects

As Cromwell told a gathering of Fifth Monarchists, the radical sects were no better than the conservative Presbyterians. His 'work', he said, was 'to preserve [the Churches] from destroying one another ... to keep all the godly of several judgements in peace, because like men falling out in the street [they] would run their heads one against another'. He described himself as 'a constable to part them, and keep them in peace'. Frustration turned to despair. A year later he complained that

'The wretched jealousies that are amongst us, and the spirit of calumny, turns all into gall and wormwood'.

Nayler's case

Cromwell, therefore, faced an uphill struggle to defend the vision of liberty of conscience he believed to be enshrined in the constitution. Parliament, in particular, remained a constant threat to the delicate balance he was trying to achieve. He may have shared MPs' abhorrence of the ideas of some of the sects such as the **Quakers**, but his fear was that, if allowed to legislate on matters of belief, they would be just as hostile to Independent and Baptist opinions. That was why Nayler's case (page 77) concerned him so much. Might not, he asked a meeting of army officers at the time, 'the Case of James Nayler ... happen to be your own case?'

KEY TERM

Quakers believed that each individual had a personal relationship with God who communicated with them directly. They therefore followed the promptings of their own inspiration, or 'inner light', rather than the teachings of ministers. This often led them to tremble or 'quake'. Since their obedience was to be given to God alone, they rejected all earthly authority, both of Church and state. They interrupted Church services, and refused to pay tithes, take oaths, or take off their hats as a mark of respect to their social superiors. The movement began in the 1650s under the leadership of George Fox. By 1660 its numbers had grown to about 50,000.

---

4 The limits of liberty

The Instrument of Government

The Instrument of Government stated that 'such as profess faith in God by Jesus Christ (though differing in judgement from the doctrine, worship or discipline publicly held forth) shall not be restrained from, but shall be protected in, the profession of the faith, and exercise of their religion ...'

It went on to make clear that liberty of conscience was not to be extended to everybody. Excluded were those who:

- practised 'Popery' (i.e. Roman Catholics);
- believed in 'Prelacy' (i.e. Anglicans wanting a Church governed by bishops);

◢ used their religious freedom to restrict the civil liberties of other people, particularly by disturbing the public peace;

◢ held beliefs which led them to behave in a 'licentious', or immoral, way.

The sects

The last two exclusions reflected concern about the activities of some of the sects which had risen up in the wake of the civil wars. The sects shared a hostility of the idea of a national Church and a distrust of the spiritual authority of ministers. They also shared a faith in the importance of each individual seeking God in his or her own way. Groups such as the **Ranters** and Quakers took the Puritan notion of a personal relationship with God to extremes, in particular using it to justify sexual permissiveness. The Quakers' theory of 'inner light' led them to reject social conventions and thus appear to threaten social order. The activities of both groups frequently led to riots and disorders, often initiated by people hostile to them.

KEY TERM

Ranters believed that God made Himself known as a divine spirit working within each individual. They denied the need for an organised Church and ministers and rejected the authority of the Bible. They believed they were chosen by God and that by following their own inner promptings they could do no wrong.

Blasphemies

Both groups held opinions which Puritans regarded as blasphemous. Cromwell agreed. Although he questioned Parliament's right to intervene in the case of the Quaker, James Nayler, he had no doubt that Nayler's opinions were to be condemned. He was heard to say privately that the Instrument 'was never intended to bolster up blasphemies of this nature'. He told petitioners on Nayler's behalf that he 'asserts from the letter of the Scriptures such things as are contrary to the common principle's written in every man's heart'.

Narrowing the limits

The problem was that the Instrument did not make clear what the 'common principles written in every man's heart' actually were. Significantly, Cromwell praised the Humble Petition and Advice which placed opinions such as Nayler's beyond the limits of acceptable belief and called for a Confession of Faith to be drawn up in order to clarify the matter still further. Although the Confession of Faith was never produced, the Humble Petition itself expanded the definition of heresy for Cromwell recognised that the idea of 'liberty of conscience' would fall into disrepute unless its limits were made clearer.

5 How far did 'liberty of conscience' extend in practice?

Cromwell clearly believed that there were limits to liberty of conscience. Yet, in practice, many who were meant to be excluded appear to have enjoyed a degree of freedom of worship under the Protectorate.

The Jews

In 1655 the Council discussed an application for Jews to be re-admitted to England for the first time since the thirteenth century. Although the application was rejected, Cromwell allowed the Jews unofficial entry. His motives were partly economic since the Jews brought considerable commercial benefits with them, and partly religious. Cromwell believed a biblical prophecy that the Jews would one day be converted to Christianity. He also believed this conversion might happen in England which God clearly regarded as His 'chosen nation'. Obviously a prerequisite was that the Jews should be able to enter the country. Again this was not an issue of toleration but one of unity among God's people.

Roman Catholics

Cromwell allowed Catholics to attend services in the chapels of foreign embassies in London. He appears to have discouraged the harsh implementation of laws against Catholics, leaving many free to worship in private.

Anglicans

Some Anglicans felt able to attend the Puritan service in their parish church. A few Anglican priests were admitted as ministers to the National Church by the Triers (see page 90). Others who wanted to use the banned Book of Common Prayer were often able to do so in private.

Radical sects

Although Cromwell believed many of their beliefs to be wrong he did not go out of his way to prevent the more radical sects from worshipping.

Political expediency or principle?

Cromwell undoubtedly had political reasons for turning something of a blind eye to the activities of Roman Catholics and Anglicans. A letter he wrote to Cardinal Mazarin of France suggests that his attitude towards Catholics was coloured by a desire to please the French government. Equally Cromwell needed to win the support of Royalists, and many Royalists were Anglicans.

Political expediency does not, however, fully explain Cromwell's extensive personal contacts among Anglicans and sectarians, his protest against the execution of a Jesuit priest or his personal interventions to secure the release of imprisoned Quakers. It seems likely that at heart Cromwell held a broader view than most of his contemporaries about the kind of people God was prepared to save. He was prepared to recognise piety in individuals of many persuasions and the possibility of salvation where others could see only error.

Cromwell's Church

1 Aims

In each parish Cromwell wanted to:

- achieve unity among Protestants who held all the essential beliefs and disagreed only about what he regarded as inessential details;
- promote teaching and preaching so that the majority of people who were not yet 'saved' would at least lead disciplined lives and at best might experience a Puritan 'conversion' and become one of the Saints.

2 Objectives

Cromwell believed that the best way to achieve these aims was to have a National Church maintained by, and responsible to, the government. Within this each congregation would have the right to run its own affairs and worship in its own way. His objectives were:

- to allow everyone who held the essential Protestant beliefs to worship freely;
- to make sure that ministers were of a high standard and would set a strong example in their personal and spiritual lives;
- to make sure they were adequately paid.

3 Methods

To implement his aims Cromwell:

◢ promoted freedom of worship (pages 83–89);

◢ ensured that there was no requirement for churches to use a common form of service or a common prayer book;

◢ in March 1654, with his Council of State, issued an ordinance setting up a commission with the job of ensuring that suitable ministers were appointed to Churches. The Triers were to assess candidates on the basis of their spiritual lives, behaviour, knowledge and ability to preach. The 38 members were carefully balanced between Presbyterians, Independents and Baptists;

◢ in August 1654, with his Council, issued an ordinance setting up commissions in each county to remove unsuitable ministers. The Ejectors were to get rid of ministers guilty of 'ignorance, insufficiency, scandal in their lives and conversations or negligence in their respective callings and places';

◢ insisted that the tithe system of paying priests, much criticised by the sects, should be kept until a better system could be found. In fact no satisfactory alternative emerged;

◢ continued the Rump's policy of using the proceeds from land that had belonged to bishops to boost the payment of ministers in the parishes where tithes were low.

4 Results

The Saints were a small minority in the country as a whole. Considering that Cromwell hoped they might create a 'godly reformation' among the great majority, his methods were fairly low key. There was, for instance, no national programme of teaching and preaching led by Puritan missionaries. Cromwell put his faith in the power of God working through godly individuals in each parish. How successful was this? More research is needed into what went on a parish level during the Protectorate, but it appears that while aspects of Cromwell's policy had some success, overall it fell far short of its aims.

Successes

◢ The system of Triers and Ejectors almost certainly did lead to high standards among ministers. According to the Puritan minister Richard Baxter, the commissioners 'saved many a congregation from ignorant, ungodly, drunken teachers ... so great was the benefit above the hurt which they brought to the Church, that many thousands of souls blessed God for the faithful ministers whom they let in, and grieved when the Prelatists afterwards [at the Restoration] cast them out again ...'.

◢ A few parishes were dominated by the Saints and run on 'godly' lines.

◢ There was a wide degree of freedom of worship.

Failures

◢ In most parishes the Saints remained a small minority.

◢ Attendance at church on Sundays remained voluntary under the Protectorate. While some people continued to attend whatever form of Puritan service was on offer from their minister in the parish church, recent research suggests that the vast majority of people would have preferred the old Anglican services.

◢ Freedom of worship and godly ministers did not lead to unity among Protestants as Cromwell had hoped. At parish level membership of sects increased rather than decreased. Cromwell's Church produced the very opposite of his intention: not unity but diversity.

The reformation of manners

1 Aims

Cromwell wanted godly ministers and godly JPs to work together to establish Christian behaviour and social discipline in every parish. They were to make sure that no sports, games or entertainments took place on Sundays and to wage war on drunkenness, swearing and sexual immorality. The resulting 'reformation of manners' would help to lead each individual towards an inner, spiritual, reformation and, thus, towards the personal relationship with God which was at the heart of the Saints' religious experience.

2 The programme of reform

Godly JPs had been attempting to reform behaviour since the sixteenth century. In 1644 Parliament tried to boost their efforts with the issue of an ordinance about what people could do on Sundays. Work, travel, buying and selling, *church ales*, feasts, dancing and games were all banned. The Rump then passed an Act making these rules even stricter, and other Acts against adultery and blasphemy. Cromwell made two particular efforts to enforce these laws at a local level:

- the system of Triers and Ejectors was intended to put in place godly ministers who would teach and enforce moral behaviour in their parishes;
- the Major-Generals (pages 75–76) were expected to:
  a) intensify the work of the Triers and Ejectors;
  b) enforce 'the laws against drunkenness, blaspheming and taking the name of God in vain by swearing and cursing, plays and interludes, and profaning the Lord's Day . . .'.

KEY TERM

Church ale was a festival linked to the religious calendar and held in a church or church-yard. It generally included a feast and various entertainments.

3 Results

Cromwell claimed that the Major-Generals were more 'effectual towards the discountenancing of vice and settling religion' than anything done for 50 years; but historians disagree with him. Research suggests that the Puritan programme to reform manners failed almost completely and that even the Major-Generals made little impact except in a few areas where they had especially strong support from local gentry. On the whole ale-houses remained in business, patterns of sexual behaviour remained much as usual and local festivals and customs either continued or revived after the Restoration. The main effect of the programme appears to have been to create resentment against a régime which threatened to destroy many of the celebrations and entertainments whereby people maintained a sense of community and well-being in their various localities. The restoration of the monarchy was welcomed partly because it marked the removal of official hostility to valued traditional ways of life.

Social reform

Aims

Cromwell's idea of a 'godly nation' included the notion that the wealthy had a responsibility to look after the needs of the many poor people who owed them obedience. As he wrote after the Battle of

Dunbar, 'If there be any that makes many poor to make a few rich that suits not a Commonwealth'. He believed that 'godly rule' was about fairness as well as discipline. His contact with his soldiers during the civil wars convinced him that afterwards they deserved to live in a fairer society. He believed this could be achieved by:

1 reforming the system of the law to make it simpler and cheaper and therefore more accessible to the common people;

2 making sure that JPs enforced the existing laws that were designed to ensure social fairness.

Achievements
Cromwell repeatedly stressed the importance of law reform to his Parliaments. In 1654 an ordinance issued with his Council made the Court of Chancery easier and cheaper to use; but the cause of law reform had been discredited by the extremist minority in the Nominated Assembly, and faced obstruction from the legal profession itself. Progress was slight.

The social justice Cromwell hoped for depended, above all, on the enthusiasm and efficiency of local magistrates. Detailed research is patchy but what there is suggests that JPs dealt efficiently and fairly with the consequences of a grain shortage and with an increase in poverty. In some counties, godly JPs were especially energetic and successful. Under Cromwell local magistrates were probably at least as efficient and sometimes more so than under the early Stuarts.

The arts
Puritans were hostile to popular festivals and popular entertainments; various Puritan writers attacked mixed dancing and the theatre for some 50 years before the Civil War broke out; and, in 1642, Parliament ordered the closure of all theatres. As a result it is often assumed that Puritans disapproved of the arts in general and that the Protectorate saw the high point of that attitude. Nothing could be further from the truth. Cromwell's 'godly reformation' did not involve an attack on the arts and under the Protectorate many of them flourished.

1 Cromwell's patronage
Cromwell's love was music, a fact confirmed even by a hostile biographer who wrote that he 'entertained the most skilful in that science in

his pay and family'. In the 1650s he employed a master of music, James Hingston. In 1657, at his daughter Frances's wedding, there was 'music by 48 violins and 50 trumpets'. He also supported artists, having his portrait painted by Robert Walker (see page 6) and by Samuel Cooper.

The Interregnum was a rich period for the writing and publication of pamphlets, book and poems. Cromwell gave support to many writers and poets who worked in his civil service. JOHN MILTON and ANDREW MARVELL were already well-known poets. The poet and playwright John Dryden and the diarist Samuel Pepys were to do most of their writing after the Restoration. The ban on theatre performance remained, partly because they were associated with gatherings of Royalists; but, in 1656, the dramatist Sir William Davenant managed to get permission from the government to stage 'The Siege of Rhodes' one of the first English operas. In 1658, he staged two more of his works, 'The Cruelty of the Spaniards in Peru' and 'The History of Sir Francis Drake', both of which supported Cromwell's war against Spain.

2 Cromwell's attitudes

Cromwell did not make statements about the arts. We have to deduce his attitudes from his actions and from the opinions of those around him. He is reported as having a sense of humour and being capable of boisterous behaviour. His daughter's wedding celebrations had 'much mirth with frolics' and, significantly, 'mixt dancing'. Perhaps there is a hint here of double standards. For, at court, Cromwell allowed what he wanted to ban from the village green. Within the social elite merry making could, apparently, be trusted not to get out of hand; but among the ordinary folk these things were too linked with ungodly behaviour to be tolerated. It is sometimes assumed that Puritans made a distinction between art and life and disapproved of art because it was not 'real'. In fact, Puritans tended to approach art as they approached life. The distinction was between the serious and the trivial, the truthful and the dishonest, the life affirming and the escapist. Art, like life, could be judged by criteria such as these. Milton approved of Francis Bacon's belief that a writer should convey 'things useful to be known'. He thought plays had their place if they were instructive. Significantly, when Cromwell was to have his portrait painted he wanted it done true to life 'warts and all'.

Profiles JOHN MILTON

In the 1630s John Milton (1608–74) wrote poems and a play, 'Comus'. In the 1640s he wrote political pamphlets. He attacked bishops, defended divorce and opposed Parliament's censorship laws arguing for a free press. In 1649 he wrote a defence of the execution of the King and became Latin Secretary to the Council of State. When he started to go blind, he had to write with the help of secretaries. In 1652 he wrote a sonnet in praise of 'Cromwell, our chief of men'. In retirement after the Restoration he wrote the two long poems for which he is most famous, 'Paradise Lost' (published 1667) and 'Paradise Regained' (1671).

ANDREW MARVELL

From 1650 to 1652 Andrew Marvell (1621–78) was tutor to Sir Thomas Fairfax's daughter. In 1653 Cromwell appointed him as tutor to his ward, William Dutton. His poems include 3 in honour of Cromwell and dealing with his own feelings about the political events of the time: 'An Horation Ode upon Cromwell's Return from Ireland' (1650), 'The First Anniversary of Government under O.C.' (1655) and 'A Poem upon the Death of O.C.' (1658). In 1657 he became Milton's assistant and then succeeded him as Latin Secretary to the Council of State. In 1659 he became MP for Hull. After the Restoration he wrote satires attacking Charles II ministers and arguing for toleration for Nonconformists.

TASKS

This chapter has dealt with Cromwell's ambition to create a godly society. Here is an exercise to help you to practise using a source (see pages 80–82) and to consider one element of the chapter: Cromwell's religious policy.

Read this source and answer the questions which follow it.

◢ Source

That such as profess faith in God by Jesus Christ (though differing in judgement from the doctrine, worship or discipline publicly held forth) shall not be restrained from, but shall be protected in, the profession of the faith, and exercise of their religion; so as they abuse not this liberty to the civil liberty of others, and to the actual disturbance of the public peace on their parts. Provided this liberty be not extended to Popery nor Prelacy, nor to such as, under the profession of Christ, hold forth and practice licentiousness.

From the **Instrument of Government** *(165*

1 Explain the terms:
  a Popery
  b Prelacy.
2 What can be inferred from this source about Cromwell's position on freedom of conscience?
3 What is the value of this source for an enquiry into Cromwell's religious policy? Think about the nature of the source, its content, and its context.
4 How far was the policy laid out in this statement actually carried out?

CHAPTER SIX

WHAT WAS CROMWELL'S IMPACT ON IRELAND AND SCOTLAND?

Objectives

◢ To examine the background to Cromwell's invasions of Ireland and Scotland

◢ To understand Cromwell's attitudes and aspirations in relation to Ireland and Scotland

◢ To explore the impact of the Cromwellian régime on Ireland and Scotland.

Case study objective

◢ To investigate alternative explanations for, and judgements on, Cromwell's actions at Drogheda.

Key events

Ireland

1641   The Irish Rebellion
1642   Formation of the Catholic Confederacy
1649   Alliance of Catholics and Royalist Protestants. Proclamation of Charles II
      Commonwealth victory at Rathmines
      Cromwell arrives in Ireland. Sieges and massacres at Drogheda and Wexford
1650   Cromwell leaves Ireland
1652   Conquest of Ireland completed
      Act for the Settlement of Ireland
1654   Council of State for Ireland set up. Charles Fleetwood appointed Lord Deputy.
      Henry Cromwell appointed commander-in-chief
1655   Fleetwood leaves Ireland
1657   Henry Cromwell appointed Lord Deputy

Scotland

1643   The Solemn League and Covenant
1647   The Engagement
1648   Defeat of the Engagers at Preston Pans
      Kirk Party takes power

1649	Execution of Charles I by the English Parliament
	Proclamation of Charles II
1650	Scots defeated at Dunbar
1651	Charles II and Scots defeated at Worcester
1654	Cromwell and Council of State issue ordinance for union of Scotland with England and Ireland
1655	Council of State for Scotland set up. Lord Broghill appointed President of the Council

Ireland

Background

Irish society

In 1640 the people of Ireland could be divided broadly into four groups:

1 The Old Irish. These were descendants of the original Gaelic inhabitants of Ireland. Traditionally most were strong Roman Catholics.

2 The Old English. These were the descendants of the Normans and English who had invaded Ireland from England during the Middle Ages. They too were mostly Roman Catholics. They now saw themselves as more Irish than English.

3 The New English. These were Protestants who had settled in Ireland in the sixteenth and early seventeenth centuries, often driving the Old Irish off their lands. They were 'planters', or colonists, sent by the English government to help it to control the island. Later they were to be known as 'Old Protestants'.

4 The Ulster Scots. These were Presbyterian Scots whom James VI and I had encouraged to settle in Ulster between 1609 and 1625.

1641–49

1 The Catholic Confederacy

In October 1641 the Old Irish of Ulster rose in rebellion. They were supported by many of the Old English. Members of both groups were threatened by the recent plantations and by the increasing influence of the New English. They were united by their Roman Catholic

aith and the belief that it was under threat. In 1642 they formed the
Catholic Confederacy which, while expressing loyalty to the crown,
aimed to protect their rights to their religion, land and political
reedoms.

2 The Earl of Ormond and the Royalists

Meanwhile Charles I had appointed the Earl of Ormond to command
an army to put down the rebellion. Ormond campaigned against the
Confederacy, now widely supported throughout Ireland. When the
Civil War broke out in England, Ormond and his army remained loyal
o the King. The majority of New English also supported the Royalist
cause. In 1643, on Charles I's instructions, Ormond negotiated a truce
vith the Confederates and the King appointed him Lord Lieutenant of
reland.

3 Parliament's supporters

The King's obvious interest in doing a deal with the Confederates in
return for Catholic support in the Civil War added to the numbers of
New English who already supported the Parliamentary cause and
confirmed the hostility against him of the Presbyterian Scots of Ulster.
Both Royalists and Confederates had to defend themselves against
these pro-Parliament forces.

4 Parliament's victory

Negotiations between Ormond and the Confederates eventually collapsed. In 1647, following Parliament's victory in the Civil War,
Ormond surrendered Dublin to Parliamentary commissioners sent
from London. He then returned to England. Parliament took up the
fight against the Catholic Confederacy.

5 Ormond and the proclamation of Charles II

In 1648 Charles I's hopes for a reversal of his fortunes centred on
playing off Parliament against its own army (which now held him pris-
oner), signing an Engagement with the Scots and raising troops in
Ireland. He therefore asked Ormond to return to Ireland to negotiate
once again with the Confederates. Agreement was reached a few days
before the start of the King's trial. On the news of his execution the
Old Irish and Old English supported by the many New English
Royalists and also the Ulster Scots (who like their compatriots in
Scotland now supported the King) proclaimed Charles II as their King

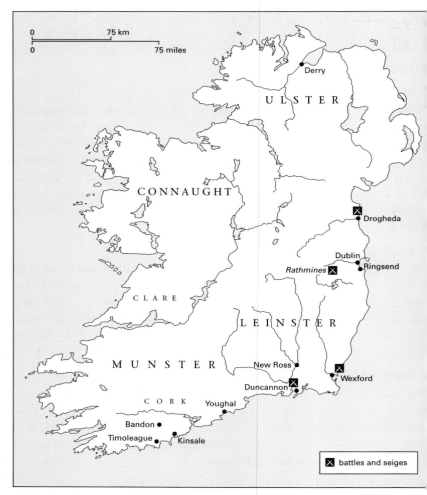

Figure 4 Cromwell's conquest of Ireland

and recognised Ormond as his Lord Lieutenant. For the first time in eight years the majority of people in Ireland were on the same side. It fell to Oliver Cromwell to try to reconquer Ireland for the new Commonwealth.

Cromwell and the conquest of Ireland

Cromwell's attitudes in 1649

Cromwell's attitude to the task ahead was dominated by three considerations:

1 Strategy

Royalist forces in Ireland posed a serious threat to the safety of the Commonwealth. He feared they might overwhelm Protestants loyal to the new republic and then invade England: '. . . we shall not only have . . . our interest rooted out there, but they will in a very short time be able to land forces in England and put us to trouble here.' That threat had to be eliminated.

2 Punishment

Like most English people Cromwell believed the false rumours that the Old Irish rebellion of 1641 had involved a carefully planned and widespread massacre of Protestants by Catholics. As he told the Irish clergy in 1650: 'You, unprovoked, put the English to the most unheard-of and barbarous massacre (without respect of sex or age) that ever the sun beheld . . . We are come to ask an account of the innocent blood that hath been shed . . . .'

Cromwell's belief was clear and it was repeated in his letters. In 1641 the Old Irish Catholics had been guilty of a terrible crime against innocent New English Protestants. Those who now resisted his army were not simply engaged in an act of political rebellion against the government of the Commonwealth. They were associating themselves with that crime of nine years before. Whether or not they could have been involved with it, they were as guilty as those who were. The Irish people were to be brought to account.

3 Obedience

That said, Cromwell also hoped to win over as many Irish people as possible to obedience to the new régime which, as he stressed, was an English régime. His declaration to the clergy ended by making it clear that his quarrel was with those priests and landowners who had, he argued, misled their followers. There was widespread fear in Ireland that Cromwell intended the extermination of the Catholic population.

This was an impression he wished to correct. To those who did not take up arms he offered a peaceable life. To those who resisted, however, he promised ruin and destruction.

The conquest

Cromwell's task in Ireland was made considerably easier by a major Parliamentary victory shortly before he and his 12,000 troops landed unopposed at Ringsend, Dublin, on 15 August 1649. At Rathmines, on 2 August, Colonel Michael Jones defeated Ormond's army as it attempted to close in on the area surrounding Dublin which he held for Parliament.

It was a decisive victory as Cromwell recognised: 'an astonishing mercy; so great and seasonable as indeed we are like them that dreamed. What can we say! The Lord fills our souls with thankfulness.' Ormond never again dared face the English army in open battle. Instead he placed garrisons in towns and castles and the war became chiefly one of sieges interspersed with small-scale engagements. It is remembered most notably for the sieges and massacres at Drogheda and Wexford (pages 106–110).

Despite setbacks including sickness among his soldiers and heavy losses in the assault of Clonmel, Cromwell managed to subdue most of eastern and southern Ireland within nine months. He was helped by divisions among his opponents and a powerful train of siege artillery which he had brought with him from England. In May 1650 he returned home leaving Ireton to continue the campaign. By 1653 the re-conquest of Ireland was complete.

Cromwell's vision in 1650

Cromwell left Ireland with ambitious ideas for its future. The country had been ravaged by nearly ten years of war. Its social structure and systems of government had collapsed. It was, he said, 'as a clean paper' and he believed it offered an unrivalled chance to build the godly society for which he believed the Civil War to have been fought and to introduce those reforms in religion and law which he wanted to see established in England. Ireland was to be a testing ground, 'a good precedent even to England itself'. Indeed success there might even make the English demand change for themselves for, 'when they once perceive propriety preserved at any easy and cheap rate in Ireland, they will never permit themselves to be so cheated and abused as now they are'.

The impact of the Cromwellian régime on Ireland

How far was Cromwell's vision fulfilled? What was the impact of his régime from 1650 to 1658?

Status

1 Dependence

Ireland had always been regarded as a dependency of England and this did not change during the time of the Republic. In 1649 Parliament proclaimed the 'Commonwealth of England and Ireland' and the Council of State sent Cromwell to Ireland with the traditional title of Lord Lieutenant. The office was temporarily abolished in 1652 and revived in 1654 when Cromwell made his son-in-law, Charles Fleetwood, his Lord Deputy.

2 Parliament

Meanwhile the Irish Parliament was abolished. Just before its own dismissal in 1653 the Rump legislated for 30 Irish MPs to sit at Westminster. Six Irish representatives were summoned to the Nominated Assembly. Under the Protectorate 30 sat in each Parliament. A Bill to unite England and Ireland was put forward in 1656 but never passed.

Land

1 English attitudes

Once the war was over the English attitude to the Irish Catholics was dominated by two factors: a desire to have revenge on those guilty of the supposed Protestant massacres and of resistance to Cromwell's army; and the need to pay for the war. Both factors pointed to the same conclusion: Irish land had to be confiscated as a punishment and given to the 'adventurers' who had put up money for the war and to the soldiers who had fought it but had still not been paid. Additionally, this would ensure the strong Protestant presence that was the best way to guarantee English control of the island in the future.

2 The 1652 Act for the settlement of Ireland

This pardoned most of the 'inferior sort' leaving their lives and property intact. Those of 'rank and quality', however, were, in a significant phrase, to be dealt with according to their 'respective demerits':

- Catholic landowners of social standing would either be executed or have their estates confiscated and be given land elsewhere of one- or two-thirds the value depending on the seriousness of their alleged crimes;
- those who had not been actively disloyal would lose one-third of their estates.

3 The consequences

In the end only a few hundred out of possible thousands were executed. About 10,000 people were transported to the West Indies or else chose to go there, and about 34,000 Irish soldiers left the country. The land confiscations and the 're-planting' of Catholics on smaller estates in the chosen areas of Connaught and County Clare proved immensely complicated. Mostly it was the landowners themselves who were re-settled, leaving their tenants in place to work for their new Protestant landlords. The result was what came to be known as the Protestant Ascendancy. Before 1641 Catholics owned 59 per cent of Irish land; by the 1660s they owned only 29 per cent. Both the Old Irish and the Old English were destroyed as political forces.

Although about 12,000 English soldiers decided to settle in Ireland, the expected emigration of thousands Protestant farmers and workers from England did not take place. Under Cromwell the future pattern of Ireland's social structure was set: Protestant landlords; Catholic tenants.

The problem of consent

1 The dilemma

Cromwell's government soon came to face the same problem in Ireland as it did in England: was it to govern by consent or force? If it was to govern by consent it had to please influential people, notably the New English, or Old Protestants as they now became known, most of whom had been Royalists. These tended to be conservative in their outlook and, therefore, opposed to radical visions and reforms. If it wanted to implement reforms the government was bound to meet with Old Protestant hostility. Consequently it would have to maintain a large army.

The trouble was, the government could not afford the upkeep of a large army. The Lord Deputy was expected to run Ireland using a combination of taxes raised in Ireland itself and a subsidy from England provided by English taxpayers. As part of a campaign to reduce expenditure Parliament cut these subsidies forcing the Lord Deputy to cut his expenditure in Ireland. That meant reducing the size of his army, but he could only do that if there was sufficient support for the régime.

2 Charles Fleetwood versus Henry Cromwell

The logic of the position was that the Lord Deputy had to pursue policies broadly supported by the Old Protestants. This Fleetwood was reluctant to do. He was a convinced Independent, keen to create a 'godly' society. Fearful that Fleetwood was alienating influential people Cromwell appointed his son, Henry, as commander-in-chief of the army and a member of Fleetwood's Council. Henry went out of his way to work with the Old Protestants. Soon he appeared to exercise more influence than Fleetwood who left Ireland in 1655. In 1657 Henry Cromwell was formally appointed Lord Deputy.

3 The consequences

The upshot was that political realities and lack of money destroyed Oliver Cromwell's hopes for reform in Ireland. No attempt was made to convert the Catholics, and Henry Cromwell ended up discouraging sectarian missionaries and encouraging priests from the Church of Ireland (the Irish equivalent of the Church of England) and Scottish Presbyterian ministers in Ulster. Even Roman Catholic priests found that they could function unchallenged provided they did not draw attention to themselves.

A brief attempt to fulfil the Cromwellian ambition of swift, cheap and impartial justice by the introduction of a new court system also foundered. The system in operation before its breakdown in 1641 was more or less restored. Recent settlers and Old Protestants loyal to the régime were appointed as JPs.

Finally, while it is true that the régime eventually brought more settled times to Ireland and even some revival in trade and prosperity, it is also the case that the government at Westminster failed to allow free trade between England and Ireland. In this respect it was no different from previous governments. The results were the same too: Irish trade and prosperity were disadvantaged. Despite the union, in the economic field as in the political, Ireland continued to be treated as a dependency of England.

Case study: Cromwell at Drogheda

The massacre at Drogheda

◢ Source 1

Cromwell reports the taking of Drogheda. This is from a letter from Cromwell to William Lenthall, Speaker of the Parliament of England, 17 September 1649.

In the heat of the action, I forbade them to spare any that were in arms in the town and I think that night they put to the sword 2,000 men ... I am persuaded that this is the righteous judgement of God upon these barbarous wretches, who have imbrued their hands in so much innocent blood*: and that it will tend to prevent the effusion of blood for the future, which are the satisfactory grounds to such actions which otherwise cannot but work remorse and regret.

*A reference to the massacres of 1641. Cromwell seems to have held all Ireland responsible. Few, if any, of those who actually took part would have been in Drogheda in 1649.

◢ Source 2

This is an extract from Cromwell's Declaration of 21 March 1650. Most of its content was addressed to the Roman Catholic Clergy. W. C. Abbott in *The Writings and Speeches of Oliver Cromwell* Volume 2 (1939) described this as 'a declaration of war to the death on the Roman Catholic Clergy and their adherents'.

You broke this union. You unprovoked, put the English to the most unheard of and most barbarous massacre.

You are part of Antichrist ... you have shed a great store of it [blood] already and ... you must all of you have blood to drink: even the dregs of the cup of the fury and wrath

of God which will be poured out unto you . . . . I shall not, where I have the power . . .
suffer the exercise of the mass . . . . If this people shall headily run on after the counsels
of their Prelates and Clergy and other leaders, I shall rejoice to exercise utmost
severity against them.

1 Comment on the value of Source 2 for a historian seeking to
explain Cromwell's actions at Drogheda.
2 What justification does Cromwell offer in Source 1 for his actions at
Drogheda?

◢ **Source 3**

This source is from Hutton, *The British Republic 1640–1660* (1990). The
incident at Drogheda has often been referred to as the great stain upon
Cromwell's reputation. But what actually happened? Nobody at the
time claimed that a single woman or child died, and most of the male
population, being unarmed, also survived.

Such behaviour was certainly more brutal than most of that during the English Civil
Wars, but how did it compare with Ireland? In 1575 . . . Sir Francis Drake called at
Rathin Island, off Ulster, to which the Macdonnells had sent their women and children
for safety. He killed all of them and reported this gleefully to his superior the Earl of
Essex, who shared his exultation. Yet nobody now seems to remember this 'stain' upon
Drake. The Catholic uprising of 1641 began with the greatest massacre of civilians
recorded in the history of the British Isles, in which at least 3,000 Protestants of both
sexes and all ages perished.

The fact that it has suited both nations to magnify the actions of Cromwell remains a
glaring example of bad history.

3 Hutton (Source 3) implies that Cromwell's reputation has been
unduly blackened. How convincingly does he advance his
argument in this extract?

◢ **Source 4**

This source is from Antonia Fraser, *Cromwell: our Chief of Men* (Mandarin,
1973).

Drogheda . . . undoubtedly frightened many lesser garrisons into peaceful submission.
Cromwell hardly needed to underline the point in his message of summons to Dundalk

soon after Drogheda, calling on them to surrender and 'thereby prevent effusion of blood'. The terrified garrison ... simply abandoned their position.

Ormonde [said] *in his letter to King Charles II: 'It is not to be imagined how great the terror is that those successes and the power of the rebels [i.e. the English] have struck into this people ... [they] are yet so stupefied that it is with great difficulty I can persuade them to act anything like men towards their own preservation.'*

Militarily, then, the sack of Drogheda could fairly be said to have done what Cromwell wanted and, what was more, the achievement came at the outset of his expedition. In September 1649 the English situation was still far from secure in Ireland for all the Rathmines victory, but Drogheda showed from the outset that Cromwell one way or another intended to be master ...

But that alas cannot be the end of the story. It is not only that the propaganda war against Cromwell in Ireland began at this point with Ormond who described the events of the sack as 'making as many several pictures of inhumanity as are contained in the Book of Martyrs'. Many and terrible were the Irish stories which grew and grew out of the fearful doings of that day and night at Drogheda: there were tales of young virgins killed by soldiers, of Jesuit priests pierced with stakes in the marketplace, of children used as shields by the assailants of the church ...

Propaganda is one thing. Personal guilt is another. It is personal guilt which interests the biographer. The conclusion cannot be escaped that Cromwell lost his self-control at Drogheda, literally saw red – the red of his comrades' blood – after the failure of the first assaults and was seized with one of those sudden brief and cataclysmic rages which would lead him later to dissolve Parliament by force and sweep away that historic bauble. There were good military reason for behaving as he did but they were not the motives which animated him at the time during the day and night of uncalculated butchery ...

And so quickly over, in the heat of the moment, in a foreign land, occurred the incident that has blackened Oliver Cromwell's name down history for over three hundred years. Even so it is important to realise that at the time the reaction to the news in England itself was one of delight and rejoicing. The ministers gave out the happy tidings from the pulpits; 30 October was set aside to be a day of public thanksgiving. More practically an additional body of troops was ordered to be sent across the Channel. All public expressions were those of satisfied acclaim: the heinous Irish rebels had received their just rewards.

◢ Source 5

This is from P. J. Cornish, 'The Cromwellian Conquest' in T. W. Moody, F. X. Martin and F. J. Byrne (eds), *A New History of Ireland* Volume III (OUP, 1991).

*By the strict rules of war, Cromwell had the right to refuse **quarter** to a town carried by a storm after reflecting a call to surrender. This was a right sparingly invoked, and in his justification of the slaughter at Drogheda it does not appear as the dominant motive ... The massacre ... became quite indiscriminate. For this he offers two lines of justification. One was policy and as policy proved only partly effective that such ruthless severity would tend to prevent the effusion of blood for the future. The second ominously was revenge ...*

The decision to surrender New Ross [19 October] without resistance might seem to indicate that Cromwell's policy of terror had begun to bite, but it was in fact dictated by tactical considerations ... His attempt to capture the great fortress of Duncannon had to be abandoned on 5 November in the face of spirited defence, and the Parliamentary troops seem to have withdrawn in some disorder. Before he was ready to leave New Ross he had the good news that Lord Broghill, his emissary to the disaffected officers in Minster had succeeded ... Officers pledged to him had seized control of Cork, Youghal, Kinsale, Bandon, and Timoleague ... The conquest [of a large area from Derry to West Cork] had been made easier by the divisions among the Royalist forces; divisions between English and Irish, between Catholic and Protestant and internal divisions between Catholics.

Study sources 4 and 5.

4 Does the treatment of Cromwell in Source 4 appear to be a sympathetic portrayal by his biographer?

5 How far does Cornish (source 5) challenge the views expressed in Source 4?

KEY TERM

Giving quarter: The rules of war provided that a commander who surrendered to a besieging enemy would be given quarter (i.e. lives would be spared). If the commander refused to surrender, he risked the lives of all who could be said to be bearing arms (i.e. civilians as well as soldiers). Once the town walls were breached by the attacker, no quarter could be sought. The rule of no quarter once the walls were breached was designed as an incentive to commanders to surrender more quickly to besiegers and, in so doing, reduce the loss of life involved.

◢ Source 6

This source is from R. S. Paul, *The Lord Protector, Religion and Politics in the Life of Oliver Cromwell* (1955).

The incidents of the Irish campaign ... cannot be considered apart from the rest of Cromwell's career. A man does not suddenly become barbarous ... there are certain factors which had become part of Cromwell's character and which became roused while he was in Ireland – distorted history, religious and national prejudices and antagonisms created or accentuated by civil wars. Undoubtedly the first of these was the horror which had been engineered in England by the exaggerated accounts of the Irish massacre of English Protestant settlers in 1641 ...

To this hatred of Ireland for one specific deed, there was added the Puritan hatred of Roman Catholicism as the system of Antichrist.

The question we must ask is not whether in the light of modern humanitarianism the massacres can be defended, but how far these actions were consistent with Cromwell's religious and moral conceptions ... we need to look at his religious and national prejudices, the standards of morality which he accepted, and the relationship between all these factors and that of military expediency.

We have already seen that Cromwell had sufficient reason for bringing the Irish campaign to a conclusion as soon as possible, and Ormond would undoubtedly try to force the invaders into a series of protracted sieges, so that the Irish weather could accomplish by sickness what he could never hope to do by force of arms ...

Perhaps a modern example will help to give us a better understanding of Cromwell at this point. In August 1945 two bombs fell on the Japanese cities of Hiroshima and Nagasaki, which according to a conservative estimate killed or maimed a total of one hundred thousand people, most of them civilians who died in circumstances of indescribable horror. The reasons given by Cromwell for the massacre of the garrison of Drogheda were precisely the same as those advanced by the Allies to justify the use of the new bomb. Although some civilians undoubtedly suffered at Drogheda the order which Cromwell gave extended only to those in arms, and on any fair assessment it would appear that he could give points in humanity to an 'enlightened' twentieth century. This is not offered in excuse for events which do blacken his name, but as an attempt to put the massacre at Drogheda into proper perspective.

Scotland

Background

1 The Covenanters

In 1560 the Scottish Parliament had set up a Presbyterian National Church, or Kirk. Despite the opposition of Kirk leaders, however, James VI had managed to become head of the Kirk and retain bishops. When, in 1637, Charles I attempted to impose the new English Prayer Book on Scotland, the majority of Scots signed a National Covenant promising to defend the Kirk. Branding them as rebels Charles I sent troops against the Covenanters. In 1639–40 they fought two wars against their King, and won. As the price of their victory Charles had to agree:

▰ to allow the Kirk to run its own affairs and abandon the new English Prayer Book;

▰ to the abolition of bishops in Scotland.

2 The Solemn League and Covenant

The Civil War divided the Scots just as it divided the Irish Protestants and the English. The majority of those in power were Covenanters who believed that the best way to secure the Kirk was to ally with the English Parliament against the King. In 1643 the Solemn League and Covenant provided for a Scots army to join Parliament's forces in England. In return Parliament agreed to set up a Presbyterian Church in England similar to that of the Kirk. Meanwhile Scotland itself experienced civil war when the Earl of Montrose led Royalists in a bloody but ultimately unsuccessful campaign against the Covenanters.

3 The Engagement

In 1646 Charles I surrendered himself to the Scots who handed him over to the English Parliament and withdrew to Scotland. There the Covenanters split. Many were angered by Parliament's failure to establish Presbyterianism in England and its refusal to acknowledge their crucial role in helping to defeat the King. The moderates, therefore, joined with the Royalists and, in 1647, formed a treaty – The Engagement – with Charles I. In return for his agreement to establish a Presbyterian Church in England for a three-year trial period, they agreed to invade England and restore him to power. In this they were opposed by a minority of hardline Covenanters, now known as the Kirk Party. In 1648 the Engagers duly invaded England where they were heavily defeated by Cromwell at Preston Pans. With Cromwell's support the Kirk Party proceeded to seize power.

4 The Kirk Party

Cromwell's hope was that the Kirk Party, whose members had been prominent in the alliance with the English Parliament during the First Civil War and hostile to Scotland's role in the Second, would form a Scottish government with which Parliament could cooperate. He misread the situation in two respects:

- the Kirk Party was even more dedicated to seeing a Presbyterian Church installed in England than the Engagers. It expected such a Church to be national and other religious beliefs to be illegal. This would not suit Cromwell and the Independents who wanted a degree of toleration and flexibility in any Church settlement.
- like all Scots, members of the Kirk Party were horrified by news of the King's execution. Charles I was, after all, King of Scotland as well as England. The English had acted without consultation. In any case the Scots were not republican-minded. They immediately proclaimed Charles II as King of *Britain*.

Cromwell's invasion of Scotland

1 The threat from Scotland

In 1650 the Kirk Party eventually managed to do a deal with its new monarch. Charles II was extremely reluctant to have anything to do with a Presbyterian Church in England. Since this was the price of active Kirk Party support for his cause, he had concentrated his hopes of invading England on Ormond in Ireland. By 1650 it was clear that Ormond had failed. Charles therefore changed tack and, in return for Scottish military support against England, reluctantly agreed to establish a Presbyterian Church in England as well as Scotland. In England the Council of State decided not to wait for the inevitable invasion. Cromwell was recalled from Ireland and given command of operations against the Scots. His instructions were to carry out a pre-emptive strike and invade Scotland.

2 Cromwell's attitudes

Cromwell's attitudes towards the Scots as he prepared to invade their

Figure 5 Scotland in the time of Cromwell

country in 1650 were very different indeed from his attitudes to the Irish as he had prepared to invade theirs the year before. The main reasons were that the Scots were not Roman Catholics and did not stand accused of the massacre of English Protestants. Like many

Englishmen he probably thought of the Scots, especially the Highlanders, as poor and barbaric like the Irish. He probably also thought of the Scots as the inhabitants of an independent state which until recently had shared a monarch with England, whereas the Irish had been made subject to England by force of arms and effectively lived in an English colony.

Over the years Cromwell's attitudes to the Scots had been on something of a switchback:

1639–40

He appears to have sympathised with their resistance to Charles I over the Prayer Book.

1643

He accepted the Solemn League and Covenant because of the need for the Scots' military help; but he was unhappy about:

1 their wish to impose a Church on England that did not allow freedom of conscience to Independents;
2 their support for the idea of negotiating with the King before he had been defeated.

1648

To the dismay of many in Parliament, Cromwell suspended military operations against the Scots after Preston Pans and backed the Kirk Party as the new government. He argued that the English quarrel was not with all Scots but with the Engagers who had restarted the Civil War. The Scots were fellow Protestants after all, and the Presbyterian Church was, in all but its attitude to freedom of conscience, a 'godly' Church. The Kirk Party which had opposed the Engagers should be given a chance and he hoped this would bring about something for which he had prayed and waited, 'union and right understanding between godly people'. 'And herein' he said, 'is a more glorious work in our eyes than if we had gotten the sacking and plunder of Edinburgh, the strong castles into our hands, and made conquest from the Tweed to the Orcades (Orkneys) . . .'

1650–51

Despite the Kirk Party's failure to live up to his hopes, Cromwell

---

again moved against the Scots in sadness rather than in fervour. He still believed them to be fundamentally 'godly', albeit misled and deluded by their leaders. 'Since we came into Scotland', he told the Speaker of Parliament, 'it hath been our desire and longing to have avoided blood in this business; by reason that God hath a people here fearing His name, though much deceived.' As he marched towards Edinburgh he issued declarations and wrote letters hoping to win over the Scots by persuasion. When that failed no victory gave him more joy or a greater conviction that God supported his cause than that of Dunbar. Afterwards, however, he continued his attempt to win over the Scots by a combination of persuasion and military pressure.

3 The campaign

The English victory at Dunbar rescued them from a perilous position. The Scots' scorched earth policy had caused the English army, reduced to 11,000 by hunger and disease, to retreat to Dunbar to receive supplies from ships. There they were hemmed in by a Scots army of 22,000. Mistakes by the Scottish commanders, Cromwell's brilliant generalship and the experience and discipline of his troops enabled a famous victory to be seized from the jaws of defeat.

Hard campaigns followed in western and central Scotland. They culminated in Charles II's invasion of England and Cromwell's overwhelming defeat of the Royalists at Worcester on 3 September 1651, the anniversary of Dunbar. General Monck remained with an army in Scotland to complete the conquest. By mid-1652 he had received the submission of all the coastal towns and the Highland chiefs.

The impact of the Cromwellian régime

1 Objectives

In 1650 the English had not set out to conquer the Scots. Their purpose was simply to persuade them to abandon their support for Charles II. When this failed conquest inevitably had to follow. The next problem was what to do with Scotland. By the time of the 1652 declaration 'concerning the Settlement of Scotland' the English had several objectives:

1 To remove the influence of those who had been responsible for 'deceiving' the Scottish people into opposition to the Commonwealth, namely:

- the King;
- the landlords who still had feudal rights over their tenants;
- the ministers of the Kirk. As Cromwell had reported, he had tried very hard to convince the Scots of the errors of their ways, 'we offered much love' but 'the Ministers of Scotland have hindered the passage of these things to the hearts of those to whom we intended them'.

2 To unite Scotland with England and Ireland in one republic.

3 To grant toleration to Independent congregations. This would introduce the twin benefits of:
- undermining the power of Presbyterian ministers;
- encouraging the spread of 'godliness'.

4 To confiscate the estates of those nobles and gentry who had supported the wars against England. The intention here was to:
- punish them;
- help to pay for the war.

5 To pardon the vassals and tenants of the leaders of the opposition and to release them from their feudal duties. Instead they would hold their land as tenants of the state, enabling them to live 'like a free People, delivered (through Gods goodnesse) from their former slaveries, vassalage and oppressions'.

2 Status

In 1651 Parliament appointed eight commissioners to run Scotland's affairs. In 1652, the commissioners offered Scottish delegates the chance to negotiate the terms of the proposed union with England. A forced union, the English claimed, would be unjust. In reality the negotiations were a sham, for the Scots had the choice of either accepting English terms for a union or rejecting them and being treated instead as a conquered people. So, although they did not want the union, they accepted it. The formalities, however, proved slow to complete. In 1654 Cromwell and his Council of State issued an Ordinance of Union. Not until 1657 did Parliament pass an Act. Meanwhile the fact of union was assumed. Scottish representatives were summoned to the Nominated Assembly and, like Ireland, Scotland sent 30 MPs to the Protectorate Parliaments.

3 Land

Between 1653 and 1655 the government had to put down a rebellion centred on the Highlands. As a result it modified its plans to destroy the power of major landowners by confiscating their lands. Instead it attempted to win them over by leniency in the hope that they would help to keep the country peaceful. So, while all feudal rights were still to be abolished (in fact, many were not), only a few landowners had their estates confiscated. The majority were fined instead, but even the fines were not always collected.

4 The problem of consent

In Scotland as in Ireland Cromwell's régime faced the problem of how far it wished, or was able, to rule by force. Here too the root of the problem was the high cost of maintaining a large army. Efforts were made to involve Scots in central and local government. In 1655 Scots were appointed to the new Council for Scotland which also included army officers and English officials. Some Scottish gentry were appointed as JPs. Over half the MPs returned to the First Protectorate Parliament were Scots. But the reality was that most influential Scots were passively hostile to the régime and did not wish to be identified with it. Only a minority served the Protectorate. The partnership Cromwell had hoped for never materialised. An English army had to remain in Scotland; and English army officers and officials remained chiefly responsible for its government.

5 Religion

Cromwell also failed in to win ministers of the Kirk over to his religious ideas. Matters were complicated by the fact that, in 1651, they had split between the majority, the Resolutioners, who continued to support the cause of Charles II, and the minority, the Protesters, who decided they no longer wished to do so. But not even the Protesters were prepared to accept Cromwellian notions of a state-controlled Church and a degree of religious toleration.

In the end the régime lowered its sights. The President of the Council, Lord Broghill concentrated on persuading both groups to minister quietly to their congregations and the Resolutioners not to offer public prayers for Charles II. In return he did not require them to declare loyalty to the Protectorate. Meanwhile the Council vetted all appointments to the Kirk. The policy of toleration appears to have led to the appearance of only a small number of Independents, Anabaptists and Quakers. Most Scots remained loyal to the Kirk.

6 Freedom and prosperity?

In theory, union with England was to release ordinary Scots from the oppression of feudal landlords and an intolerant Kirk. In practice, some feudal rights were left untouched and the Kirk continued its hold on its congregations. There is little evidence that any Scots resented this, or that many commoners felt much loyalty to the new régime. Under the Protectorate calm returned to Scotland; but taxation remained high and the majority of Scots remained poor. The traditional leaders of Scottish society, the landowners and ministers, found that they could co-exist with the Cromwellian régime; but in their hearts they harboured the grievances of a conquered people.

TASKS

Reputations in History

1 Study Source 6 (on page 110).

Do you agree that the historian must examine Cromwell's actions in the light of the standards of morality which he accepted rather than 'in the light of modern humanitarianism'?

2 Refer to Sources 3 to 6 (pages 107–110).

To what extent do differences of view about Cromwell's actions at Drogheda appear to depend on whether military expediency is viewed as part of an explanation or of a justification for Cromwell's actions?

3 Refer to Sources 1 to 6 (pages 106–110).

Hutton (Source 3) suggests that reputations in history do not always reflect accurately or fully an individual's actions. On the basis of these extracts, does Cromwell's reputation appear to have been excessively stained in portrayals of the events at Drogheda?

CHAPTER SEVEN

THE LEGACY OF OLIVER CROMWELL

Objective

◢ To assess Cromwell's achievements at the time of his death and the long-term impact of his rule.

Cromwell's achievements

Abroad

Historians debate whether Cromwell's foreign policy was primarily driven by his religious concern to create a European Protestant alliance against the old Catholic enemy, Spain, or by his concern for the nation's commercial and security interests. But as the historian Barry Coward has pointed out, the likelihood is that Cromwell and his Council dealt with foreign affairs under the kind of pressure described by the Venetian ambassador: 'They are so fully occupied that they do not know which way to turn, and the Protector has not a moment to call his own.' It is probable that rather than follow one clear-cut policy Cromwell had to respond to events as best he could, balancing political and commercial gains against religious principle as he went along.

Summary

Cromwell was chiefly concerned with four countries:

1 The United Provinces   Cromwell had opposed the Rump's Dutch War against a fellow-Protestant state. Following a British naval victory at Texel in 1653 he opened peace negotiations. At the Treaty of Westminster (1654) the Dutch agreed to end their support for the Stuart cause and to accept the 1651 Navigation Act designed to help British trade.

2 Spain   In 1654 Cromwell decided to attack Spain's Caribbean colonies. In 1655 the Western Design apparently failed when the Spaniards repelled an attack on Hispaniola; but the capture of Jamaica instead gave England its first colony in the region and proved more valuable in the long term. Later, part of a Spanish treasure fleet was also captured. In 1657, in alliance with France, the republic's army helped win victories against Spain in Flanders and captured Dunkirk.

3 France The French hoped for English help in their long-running war with Spain. Although France was a Catholic power Cromwell was drawn towards an alliance for several reasons: his own anti-Spanish feelings; the need to prevent the French from supporting the Stuarts; his good relationship with the chief Minister of France, Cardinal Mazarin; French agreement, in 1655, to put pressure on their ally, the Duke of Savoy, to stop the massacre of Protestants in the Vaudois valley.

In 1655 the two countries formed a defensive alliance and the French agreed to stop sheltering the Stuarts. In 1657 this became a military alliance against Spain.

4 Sweden Cromwell had hopes of forming an anti-Catholic Protestant alliance with Charles X of Sweden. At the same time he wanted to avoid an alliance which would give any one power dominance in the Baltic region which was becoming of central importance to English trade. In 1656 he concluded an Anglo-Swedish trading agreement but avoided a military alliance, remaining neutral in the war between Sweden and Denmark which began in 1657.

Assessment

Both contemporaries and historians have disagreed as to whether or not Cromwell's anti-Spanish and pro-French policy was in England's best interests. France was the up-and-coming European power and potentially a greater threat than Spain which was no longer the great power it had been. Also English merchants trading there complained that the war was against their interests. Clearly, however, Cromwell managed to promote England's commercial interests in the Baltic. In the decision to mount the Western Design and the government's subsequent attempts to promote the settlement of Jamaica, some historians have seen the first steps towards the creation of a trading empire.

In two respects Cromwell's dealings with foreign powers were highly successful. Firstly, he managed to neutralise the support of other states for the Stuart cause. Secondly, he made the republic universally respected abroad. Admittedly this was at a huge financial cost. The upkeep of a powerful navy was especially expensive. But there was no doubt about the outcome as the Royalist historian Clarendon made memorably plain, 'his greatness at home was but a shadow of the glory he had abroad. It was hard to discover which feared him the most, France, Spain, or the Low countries'.

At home

1 The failure of ideals

When Cromwell died he had failed to achieve many of his own objectives. Above all, he had not yet managed to find a constitutional settlement which commanded popular support. Admittedly the revised Humble Petition and Advice was a constitution proposed by Parliament; but his régime was still ultimately based on the power of the army. The National Church could boast many sound and godly ministers and many people enjoyed freedom of worship; but there was little sign of the religious unity for which Cromwell longed. Social reform was slow and patchy. Likewise the reform of behaviour which was also much resented. In both Ireland and Scotland his government had retreated from reforming policies in order to gain the support, or at least the passive acceptance, of traditional ruling groups (Chapter 6).

2 An acceptable republic?

It is important to bear in mind, however, that despite a general lack of enthusiasm for 'godly rule' and for a government behind which the glint of soldiers' swords could always be seen, Cromwell's régime had survived. Indeed it had done better than that. Although many property owners never entirely lost their fear that the freedom allowed to the radical sects might lead to social indiscipline and upheaval, the Protectorate did manage to maintain social order. By the time of his death there were even signs that Cromwell's efforts to reach out to his old Royalist opponents were meeting with modest success. Some of the traditional ruling families which had withdrawn from English local government in the early days of the republic were again becoming JPs. Republican rule may not have been popular but it was becoming acceptable, and that in itself was an achievement.

3 The collapse of the republic

As it was, the régime depended too much on the personality and authority of Cromwell himself. After his death neither his son,

Richard, nor the army generals who directed affairs after him were able to control turbulent economic and political forces. In the ensuing chaos it was an army general, George Monck, who recognised that political stability could only be achieved if the army abandoned its reforming agenda and re-established a civilian constitution. At the same time support was growing for the restoration of the monarchy. Monck's intervention led to the Restoration of 1660.

At the Restoration there was an intense reaction against Cromwell and every effort was made to discredit anything to do with his régime. It appeared that the impact of the Cromwell years was to be purely negative. How true is this?

What was the long-term impact of Cromwell's rule?

Society and government

1 Social order

In two apparently contradictory ways Cromwell's régime confirmed and strengthened the conservative social outlook of the gentry and aristocracy. His views on liberty of conscience seemingly gave encouragement to members of the radical sects whose theories and behaviour struck fear into the hearts of landowners at the head of local society. At the same time Cromwell's own words and actions stressed the importance of maintaining traditional social hierarchies. He managed both to bolster social order and to appear to threaten it. He ensured that in social terms the English revolution was not revolutionary at all, and that the aim of the propertied classes would be to ensure that there should be no further threats to their position.

2 Military rule

Despite his wish to base his régime on a civilian foundation Cromwell's commitment to godly rule tied him to military rule. The gentry were offended by detachments of soldiers stationed around the country, the high cost of maintaining them, the many officers who became JPs, the Major-Generals who threatened traditional local government and the Decimation Tax which sustained them. All this created a deep hatred of military rule and ensured that in the years to come the social elite would be hostile to standing armies.

3 Godly rule

Cromwell also helped to discredit the idea that the state should be set up and run on religious principles. Godly rule was unpopular because it meant military rule, involved interference of the majority by a minority and appeared to unleash disruptive social forces among the sects. The English became wary of religious enthusiasm in general.

4 Crown and Parliament

Did the restoration of the monarchy mean that Cromwell had no impact on the English constitution? Was the republic simply an episode to be forgotten?

The monarchy

The restored monarchy of 1660 was more limited in its powers than that of 1642; but it can be argued that the terms on which Parliament would have made peace in 1648, had Cromwell and the army not prevented it, would have left the crown weaker than in 1660. In that sense Cromwell weakened Parliament's position. It was not until the Glorious Revolution of 1688 that the balance between crown and Parliament was finally settled in Parliament's favour.

Parliament

But it was Parliament which recalled Charles II and from then on Parliament's rights within the constitution were to be recognised. Cromwell can be said to have influenced this development in two opposing ways: because at heart he did not wish to base his power on the army he kept alive the principle that Parliament had a central role to play in the constitution; in practice, however, he diminished Parliament's role by purging MPs and subordinating Parliament's authority to a 'necessity' born of his religious ambitions. In effect he ruled by his own version of divine right. This simply fuelled the conviction of the majority of gentry that the best way to avoid such absolutism was through a constitution incorporating a strong Parliament and limited monarchy.

Consent

After 1660 the monarch ruled on different terms. Charles II recognised that he had to rule with the consent of the governing classes as expressed through Parliament. James II's failure to shift the balance back towards a royal absolutism confirmed the new reality. Cromwell had contributed to this development as military leader and as one of the minority of radicals who had brought about the trial and execution of Charles I. He had helped to make the unthinkable a reality. Monarchs could be resisted and destroyed. Subsequently, Cromwell's own period of rule had confirmed that without a large degree of consent a government lacked both legitimacy and ultimate stability. Neither the governing classes nor Charles I's successors would forget this.

Religion

Cromwell's vision of a broad National Church was destroyed at the Restoration along with any notion of liberty of conscience. The restored Church of England was a narrow, intolerant Church. The 1662 Act of Uniformity required priests to take tests to prove they agreed with the Book of Common Prayer. Some 2,000 ministers had to leave their parishes when they failed because of their Puritan opinions. The laws known as the Clarendon Code denied freedom of worship to Catholics and Nonconformists and prevented them from holding office in local or national government.

It was due to Cromwell that Dissenters formed so large a group after the Restoration. He had aimed for Protestant unity but achieved diversity. His policy of liberty of conscience enabled the sects to grow, which in turn enabled them to survive the hostile pressures of the Restoration period and to continue as a small but influential minority.

England, Scotland and Ireland

Ronald Hutton has suggested that, although the British republic collapsed in 1660, Cromwell's long-term impact on Scotland and Ireland was to set the terms of their future relationship to England:

◢ Source

... it is in a British, not an English, context that the true importance of the Interregnum should be appreciated. It is not too much of an exaggeration to suggest that during the years 1649–53 the modern political relationships of the three British realms were formed. In 1660 they divided once more into three kingdoms, theoretically linked only by a crown, but there is little doubt that the balance between them had been determined by the events of the previous decade in a way that had not been done before. It was Cromwell's army which ensured that henceforth England would be clearly dominant over the other two realms.

Ronald Hutton, ***The British Republic 1649–1660*** *(1990)*

England and the world

Under Cromwell the republic defeated both the United Provinces and Spain. As a result England achieved a dominance at sea which gave her merchant ships access to every part of the trading world. This was to be the basis of her future commercial expansion.

Controversy

This book ends, where it began, with Cromwell's reputation. For among his most enduring legacies are the controversies that have raged since his own lifetime about his motives, the extent of his achievements and the nature of his significance. On the following pages you can read some of the conflicting opinions which modern historians hold about one of the most complex and fascinating figures in British history. The task is designed to help you weigh up Cromwell's achievements and reach an informed view, taking these opinions into account.

TASKS

1 Make a chart with two columns headed 'Positive achievements' and 'Negative achievements'. Read the opinions of historians that follow. Identify what they consider to be Cromwell's positive and negative achievements and enter these on your chart.

For Christopher Hill there are two Cromwells: the one a breaker with conventions and defender of liberties; the other a conservative figure who repressed the progressive forces he had unleashed.

◢ Source

If we emphasise the 1640s we can with Marvell see Oliver Cromwell as 'the force of angry heaven's flame', an elemental power cleaving its way through all opposition 'to ruin the great work of time, and cast the kingdom old into another mould'. Or we can see him as the fiery protagonist of greater liberty of thought and opportunity, hostile to dogmatism, privilege and shams. If on the other hand we dwell on Cromwell's suppression of the Levellers and his subsequent uneasy career, he appears an all-too-human class-conscious conservative, a wily politician using all his arts to preserve a hated military régime – and as the founder of the British Empire.

Christopher Hill, **God's Englishman** (1971)

J. P. Kenyon argues that Cromwell damaged the Parliamentary cause and condemned the country to an unnecessarily drawn out continuation of the constitutional struggle between Parliament and crown:

◢ Source

Cromwell's character remains very much an enigma, but it is clear that much of the praise lavished on him then and later is misplaced. In the early 1650s he alone stood between the English people and a peaceful and permanent settlement; without his leadership and military genius, the republic would have foundered in its first two years; single-handed he postponed the inevitable restoration of the monarchy for another ten. Moreover, his increasing authoritarianism so weakened the cause for which he had struggled that after his death his bewildered and demoralised successors had to recall Charles II on his own terms, without imposing on him conditions which would have made the introduction of authoritarian government impossible and the Revolution of 1688 unnecessary.

J. P. Kenyon, **Stuart England** (Penguin, 1985)

TASKS

Finally, Ronald Hutton acknowledges that Cromwell may have had the best interests of the nation at heart but stresses that 'he was also a practical politician who yielded to necessities':

◢ Source

Repeatedly he would strive for compromise, but as soon as an event appeared inevitable, such as the regicide or the dissolution of the Purged Parliament, he would seize control of the process and so reassert his influence. In the last analysis, he never forgot that his power depended on pleasing the army. Defenders of Cromwell would suggest that at such times he was waiting to see which way the will of God was tending and then following it. Perhaps he was, but then God clearly always wanted Cromwell to survive politically. Like any politician, he manipulated people and he told half-truths: a reading of his speeches easily illustrates how he remoulded the memory of past events to serve present needs, and altered his persona (squire or saint) to suit his audience. He was by nature expansive, emotional and good-humoured, and employed these attributes as assets, knowing well when to submit others to an outburst of fury, a flight of rhetoric or some boisterous bonhomie. Again personality and tactic are impossible to distinguish. To say that he aimed at power would be horribly unjust, but he did have a shrewd instinct for retaining it.

Ronald Hutton, ***The British Republic 1649–1660*** *(1990)*

2 The poet Andrew Marvell wrote these lines in 'An Horation Ode upon Cromwell's Return from Ireland' in 1650:

'Tis Madness to resist or blame
The force of angry Heavens flame:
And, if we would speak true,
Much to the Man is due.
Who, from his private Gardens, where
He liv'd reserved and austere ...
Could by industrious Valour climbe
To ruine the great Work of Time,
And cast the Kingdome old
Into another Mold.

Do you think that, in the end, Cromwell did 'cast the kingdom old into another mould'?

FURTHER READING

Books marked * are recommended as starting points.

Biographies

*Barry Coward *Oliver Cromwell* (Longman, 1991)

C. H. Firth *Oliver Cromwell and the Rule of the Puritans in England* (OUP, 1990)

Christopher Hill *God's Englishman* (Weidenfeld and Nicolson, 1971)

Robert S. Paul *The Lord Protector* (Lutterworth Press, 1955)

Surveys

G. E. Aylmer *Rebellion or Revolution? England 1640–1660* (OUP, 1987)

T. Barnard *The English Republic* (Longman, 1982)

*Barry Coward *Stuart England, 1603–1714* (Longman, 1997)

Derek Hirst *Authority and Conflict: England 1603–1658* (Edward Arnold, 1987)

R. Hutton *The British Republic, 1649–1660* (Macmillan, 1990)

*Michael Lynch *The Interregnum 1649–1660* (Hodder and Stoughton, 1994)

Austin Woolrych *England without a King, 1649–1660* (Lancaster pamphlet, Methuen, 1983)

Collections of essays

G. E. Aylmer (ed.) *The Interregnum: the Quest for Settlement* (Macmillan, 1973)

John Morrill (ed.) *Reactions to the English Civil War, 1642–49* (Macmillan, 1982)

John Morrill (ed.) *Oliver Cromwell and the English Revolution* (Longman, 1990)

John Morrill (ed.) *Revolution and Restoration: England in the 1650s* (Collins and Brown, 1992)

I. Roots (ed.) *Cromwell: A Profile* (Macmillan, 1973)

Collections of documents

Ivan Roots (ed.) *Speeches of Oliver Cromwell* (Dent, 1989)

*David L. Smith *Oliver Cromwell: Politics and Religion in the English Revolution, 1640–1658* (CUP, 1991)

*H. Tomlinson and D. Gregg *Politics, Religion and Society in Revolutionary England, 1640–1660* (Macmillan, 1989)